KYOTOPOLIS

KYOTOPOLIS

A Play in Two Acts

Daniel David Moses

Exile Editions

Publishers of singular
Fiction, Poetry, Non-fiction, Drama, and Graphic Books

2008

Library and Archives Canada Cataloguing in Publication

Moses, Daniel David, 1952-
Kyotopolis / Daniel David Moses.

A play.
ISBN 978-1-55096-116-4

1. Indians of North America--Drama. I. Title.

PS8576.O747K96 2008 C812'.54 C2008-905966-2

Design and Composition by Digital ReproSet
Cover Digital Composite by Jayeson Earl
Typeset in Garamond at the Moons of Jupiter Studios
Printed in Canada by Gauvin Imprimerie

The publisher would like to acknowledge the financial assistance of the Canada Council for the Arts and the Ontario Arts Council, which is an agency of the Government of Ontario.

Conseil des Arts du Canada
Canada Council for the Arts

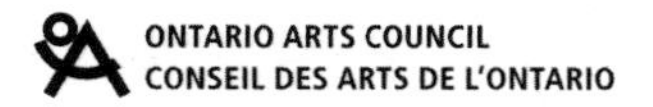

Published in Canada in 2008 by Exile Editions Ltd.
144483 Southgate Road 14
General Delivery
Holstein, Ontario, N0G 2A0
info@exileeditions.com
www.ExileEditions.com

Canadian Sales Distribution:
McArthur & Company
c/o Harper Collins
1995 Markham Road
Toronto, ON M1B 5M8
toll free: 1 800 387 0117

U.S. Sales Distribution:
Independent Publishers Group
814 North Franklin Street
Chicago, IL 60610
www.ipgbook.com
toll free: 1 800 888 4741

When the bough breaks, the cradle will fall,
And down will come baby, cradle and all.

—EFFIE CROCKET, *Rockabye Baby*

...I went around the world inside a big trout...
So I wasn't too surprised when I got on that
Air Canada jet.

—RON GEYSHICK, *Te Bwe Win: Truth*

KYOTOPOLIS

CHARACTERS (in order of appearance)

BABE Fisher (a little Indian girl)

CLARISSE Chrisjohn (an Indian street worker)

JACK Buck (BABE's great uncle)

BARBARA Buck (BABE's great aunt)

MARTHA Fisher (BABE's grandmother)

BOO Fisher (BABE's aunt)

TOMMY Hawk (Indian clown, host of a children's television show)—is later also RICKY Raccoon, as well as the LADY in black and cameraman NICKY

MARY Oh (virtuo jockey/rogue reporter)—is later also the SISTER, a nun in black

LARRY (MARY's cameraman) the voice of launch CONTROL

JO (MARY's producer)

Fred FACE, the reporter

Curly BEAR (CLARISSE's husband)

the TWO RANGERS

a female ANGEL

the voice of the Tele Presence SYSTEM

a Tele Presence OPERATOR

BEAVER (a puppet)

the Chocolate MOOSE (a puppet)

L.A. CHIEF of police Harry Smith

The play is set at a variety of intersections in the global Indian village, that almost-present dream of the city of tomorrow. Straight paths cross circular ones, ideas meet pleasure, directions become dimensions, and the news meets an old or other story, all in a play of light across and through and in and out of the open face of the planet.

ACT ONE, SCENE ONE

Darkness.

Then a drum begins an extremely slow double-beat, like a heart from far off in a dream. And with each heartbeat there's a pulse of light projecting a place. First it's a cracked rock face covered with petroglyphs—highly abstracted images of men, women, boats, bears, turtles, Nanabush. Then it's a city seen at night from the air with a freeway a glowing blur. Then it's the Milky Way—and the nearby constellations are very clear. And then it's a path through a clearing.

And then the cycle of these four places begins again. And it becomes clear that the crack in the rock, the freeway and the Milky Way are all somehow the path through the clearing, because along it, along them, comes BABE, *a little Indian girl, dawdling in the pulsing lights, trailing a red balloon on a string, paying attention to Nanabush, or stars, or cars, or yellow butterflies.*

And then, as the cycle begins once more, away from the path but in the half-light of petroglyphs and then constellations and then apartments and then leaves, CLARISSE *and* JACK, *and then* BARBARA *and* MARTHA, *and then* BOO *and* TOMMY *(as a face on a monitor), and then* RICKY, *appear and turn (even* TOMMY *from the monitor) to face* BABE, *to watch her.*

And then, as the heartbeats come more quickly, BABE *tries a few steps of a powwow dance, probably a jingle dance, maybe a shawl dance, and so loses her hold on the balloon. The drum hesitates and all the lights but the path fade down. And the balloon lifts away and* BABE*'s eyes follow it with longing. Then someone, something, somewhere ahead—perhaps the drum which now begins to insistently beat—calls her and she hurries off along the fading path with one last look back and up.*

And the drum becomes a strange background rumbling and the progress toward the sky of the balloon stops, fades to the stars. And as the stars fade with the coming dawn, the rumbling shifts into distant surf and present insects.

MARY: Oh...

LARRY: Are you all right? You phased out there for a sec.

MARY: What? I did not. It's this stupid equipment, okay? Hello? Hello? Is it on now?

(The unit's light flares up and MARY *Oh turns toward its spot)*

MARY: We've got the power now? Okay?

(Her cameraman LARRY *gestures toward her earpiece)*

MARY: I can't hear a thing.

LARRY: Careful there, Mo.

MARY: What is it? What?

LARRY: You're about to slip into the Banana River.

MARY: Larry, I thought you if anyone would know that this is the Indian—oh—*(she slips and falls to her knees)*—sugar.

LARRY: I don't care about geography, Mo.

MARY: Stay where you are, okay, there's no time.

LARRY: You jogged the hookup.

MARY: But I hear something now. And this is the Indian River. The Banana's the one behind you.

LARRY: Why aren't we covering this from the inside like human beings?

MARY: Just don't shoot my knees.

LARRY: They don't got mud in there, Mary.

MARY: *(touching her earpiece)* Quit bugging me. Hello, Jo? Jo! What the H is going on? We don't want to miss this, okay?

LARRY: But we're out here in the sanctuary with all the animals.

MARY: You're not much of an Indian, Larry.

LARRY: Me certified Injun-eer. 'Sides, this is Seminole country.

MARY: Are all the Delaware so delicate?

LARRY: Piss off, little miss.

MARY: Language like that won't get you far in show business.

(LARRY *makes a raspberry)*

MARY: Okay okay, quiet. Here comes the feed.

(Her monitor snows on)

MARY: That's more like it.

LARRY: You wouldn't be such a bitch if you ate properly.

MARY: I fast as a gesture of respect, okay?

LARRY: And I thought you was anorexic.

MARY: Shut up, you idiot, we're back.

(The image of MARY *Oh reporting comes on the monitor)*

MARY: Good morning, everyone. This is Mary Oh, here beside the Indian River—

LARRY: Enterprise Two—

MARY: —in the Merritt Island International—

LARRY: —Columbia Three.

MARY: —Wildlife Sanctuary—

LARRY: Discovery—

MARY: —to bring you—

LARRY: —Atlantis—

MARY: —a really special perspective—

LARRY: —Endeavour.

MARY: —on today's launch of the Crazy Horse space shuttle.

LARRY: Crazy Horse.

(The strange rumbling returns, now through the monitor)

LARRY: Why not?

MARY: They tell me that we can expect a resumption in the countdown just about any time now.

LARRY: But there's one missing.

MARY: Countdown got stopped at tee minus thirty. That was just fifteen minutes ago. But launch control doesn't want to miss this window of opportunity?

LARRY: *(touching his earpiece)* Jo, isn't there supposed to be some animation cut in here?

MARY: They tell me they had to check out something called an anomaly in one of the many, many computer programs that control the shuttle's trajectory?

LARRY: How do you mean we can't afford it?

MARY: This shuttle is the very first shuttle ever named after a Native American.

LARRY: What do you mean, they'll catch us?

MARY: What a gesture of recognition of what Amerindians have given our civilization! And we're talking more than Thanksgiving turkey! We're talking about now.

(On the monitor, cut-away to a distant shot of the shuttle awaiting launch in the midst of the surrounding swamp land. A red sunrise light begins to be evident, both on the monitor and on MARY *and* LARRY*)*

LARRY: So they don't know we're here?

MARY: We're talking about tomorrow. It's a red-letter day for the International Space Program. Okay?

LARRY: She what?

MARY: All the ladies and gents from all the countries in the international space accord agree.

LARRY: I can't believe her.

MARY: I mean everybody I talked to here today at the launch facility says that the time has come.

LARRY: Our Miss Oh.

MARY: I'm just so excited and honoured to be reporting from the Kennedy Centre today, everyone, for there is, as you are all aware, a reason that this flight is more than a gesture.

LARRY: Oh, she's babbling now, Jo.

MARY: This launch is historic, a realization of a dream.

LARRY: Shit, I don't know. The national anthem?

MARY: Today marks the climax of a meteoric and fascinating career, and we're witnessing here a triumph both personal and social. Yes, the presence on this mission into space of an aboriginal person, Special Flight Officer Babe Fisher, one of the first Americans—

LARRY: Jo, they'd be grateful if we cut away to the game.

MARY: —testifies not only to her own achievements as an explorer of the spiritual realm but also to the efforts of the New Age Party.

LARRY: I'd be grateful if we cut away to the game.

MARY: Because of their forward-looking Toward Utopia campaign, the Babe, shamaness extraordinaire, is now the advisor to the mission commander.

LARRY: Not that grateful.

(The image of MARY *Oh comes back onto the monitor)*

MARY: And the commander has declared that the New Age Plan has revitalized the space program.

LARRY: This is embarrassment like embodied.

MARY: Mizz Fisher, or the Babe as we all know her, prepared for this flight through her own regimen of cleansing rituals—including fasting—and is supposed to enter a trance sometime tomorrow.

LARRY: I could pass for Mexican, *si?*

MARY: Other flight specialists are going to conduct experiments into the effects of zero gravity on such established paranormal practices as crystal growing, telekinesis and telepathy.

LARRY: You teach me some Spanglish, maybe?

MARY: It is hoped that the space program can use intuitive insights gained from the Babe's shamanic journey to reify observations made on previous flights about the organic unity and corporeal intelligence of our planet and finally make it possible to live on the Moon Two space station.

(The monitor cuts back to the distant shot of the shuttle awaiting launch. The camera zooms in as the shuttle begins to exhaust)

LARRY: *Madeira de Dios!* What's that mean?

MARY: Oh, I think now of the words of the song in Babe Fisher's wonderful virtual reality disc *Ode to the Blue*

Mother. How they've moved us all so much with images of the opalescent magic of the earth. We don't have time to play that virtuo here—

LARRY: Ya? Finally.

MARY: —but it is featured all this week on my *V. D. Oh Show*, virtually the best to you—

LARRY: Shit, listen to your feed!

MARY: Okay, everyone, okay. The countdown's resumed. We are at tee minus ten and counting. Okay!

(Smoke drifts by through the yellowing light)

CONTROL: *(over)* Tee minus nine. Tee minus eight. Tee minus seven.

MARY: Oh, Larry, Larry, look.

CONTROL: *(over)* —Tee minus six.

LARRY: You're still live!

CONTROL: *(over)* —Tee minus five. Four. Three. Two. One! We have ignition! We have liftoff!

MARY: *(watching the monitor)* The shuttle Crazy Horse rises majestically on its pillar of fire into the heavens.

(More smoke, enough to black out the sunlight)

MARY: From here in the Floridian wetlands, it's quickly becoming our star in the daylight sky, a star shot into the new frontiers in our search for harmony. Look at it go, boys!

(The monitor shows a cloudy sky now)

MARY: *(peering skyward)* That twinkle of our star means, I believe, that the burn of the twin solid rocket boosters is complete and the tank has been jettisoned.

(The smoke begins to clear)

MARY: It will fall to earth down range from here.

(The monitor cuts back to MARY *reporting)*

MARY: The orbiter's three main engines should now be burning? That will thrust the Crazy Horse to the edge of space and to near-orbital velocity.

(A flash of lightning bright light)

MARY: What's that?

(The monitor cuts back to the cloudy sky)

LARRY: Holy shit.

(A heartbeat)

MARY: What? What?

LARRY: There's been an explosion. Just as they were going into orbit.

MARY: But that's when the engines shut down. It's just like before—

LARRY: The Challenger.

MARY: Oh, God, it's like the Challenger all over again. Oh, my God!

LARRY: The one I forgot.

MARY: What's the news? Jo? Jo? What's going on?

LARRY: Blew another shitty gasket.

MARY: The Crazy Horse orbiter has survived the explosion but, oh, there's no communication from the crew.

(The monitor goes dark)

MARY: I'm sorry, everyone, but my feed from the Space Centre has been cut off. We'll get the news to you as soon as possible. I wonder if she's okay.

*(*LARRY *gestures a finger across his throat)*

MARY: What? She can't be dead. Was it the shock of the blast? They—the crew of the shuttle, including Barbara 'Babe' Fisher—oh my God, they're dead.

(JO, wearing a headset, enters. More smoke)

JO: You're off the air, young lady.

MARY: Tell me what happened.

JO: I wish I'd never let you talk me into this. There's been an explosion.

MARY: I know that, you idiot.

JO: In the booster rockets.

MARY: But what about the orbiter?

LARRY: They were still too close.

JO: The blast pushed them into orbit but the shuttle's spinning out of control.

(The sound of an approaching, airborne whistling, like a bomb)

LARRY: What the fuck is that?

JO: The orbit's unstable.

MARY: How could this happen?

JO: The booster rockets disintegrated into shrapnel.

(A large piece of metallic debris crashes horrendously to earth nearby. They panic. Lots more smoke)

JO: I'm out of here.

MARY: What's going on? What's going on?

LARRY: Come on, Mo.

JO: *(exiting)* Never again.

LARRY: Come on, let's get out of here!

MARY: What's going on?

LARRY: This is shit.

MARY: What's going on? *(she faints)*

(The lights drop down to her and then to darkness. The drum heartbeats once)

ACT ONE, SCENE TWO

(And out of the darkness and the heartbeating drum comes the pulsing, projected night city where CLARISSE *stands in the half-light)*

CLARISSE: Like it looked alive and I remember I wondered if it was like holding its breath or maybe was just moving slow so I couldn't tell for sure in them shadows. Like them cracks was opening up like mouths. Like the mouth of that baby.

(Another heartbeat brings up a light on MARY. *Then the night city and* CLARISSE *disappear in the dark as the monitor blares on in the middle of a live report)*

FACE: —where we are standing outside the Fisher Community Entertainment Centre on the New Nations Reserve—

(Mid-morning light comes up on Fred FACE, *the reporter, being shot by cameraman* LARRY. MARY*'s watching from off to one side)*

FACE: —a facility that was a donation from that celebrated young woman in whose memory the service today was held. It is our profound hope that we be allowed a few words with members of her family.

MARY: He's blowing the story, okay?

FACE: —Perhaps they can help us put into perspective the young Barbara Fisher's demise only two days ago as a member of the ill fated Crazy Horse crew.

It is this tragedy that has so shocked the world that the assassination of the original Crazy Horse himself has been invoked in a search for an historical parallel. It is with the most heartfelt sympathy for their loss that we today have joined the members of the New Nations band.

MARY: Look look look.

(Enter TOMMY *Hawk, in a clown's tuxedo for mourning, at a run)*

MARY: Fred!

FACE: And here comes someone—

LARRY: *(touching his earpiece)* That's Tommy Hawk, Jo.

(A heartbeat)

FACE: Excuse me, sir, sir, are you connected with the family? It is Mister Hawk, ladies and gentlemen, Mister Thomas Hawk. Sir! Could you speak with us?

TOMMY: Me? You?

FACE: Yes—

TOMMY: No. I mean well—who's he?

FACE: That's Larry.

TOMMY: That's Larry? Peekaboo!

FACE: It is Mister Hawk?

TOMMY: Oh, lady! Peekaboo to you too.

FACE: Mister Hawk, please we're—

TOMMY: We're late, I'm sorry, we're very late!

FACE: Sir, please—

TOMMY: Got a plane to catch.

FACE: —we need to hear from you.

TOMMY: Catch you later. See you later, alligator. Adios. Can't wait.

(exiting)

MARY: He recognized me!

FACE: Well, it seems clear, ladies and gentlemen, that Mister Hawk, like all of us, is having some difficulties right now—

MARY: The Chocolate Moose!

FACE: —dealing with the tragic ramifications of this tragic.

MARY: The children's show!

FACE: *(listening to his feed)* —It was Mister Hawk, of course, who first brought Barbra 'the Babe' Fisher to public attention. It was as 'baby Barbie', the youngest member of the troupe of kids populating the preschool program *Tommy Hawk and the Little People* that Babe helped establish Native culture programming on satellite television worldwide.

MARY: Jo knows I could have got that interview.

FACE: *Tommy Hawk and the Little People* is an internationally registered trademark of Big Buck Productions and the program is still produced and distributed by that company from a studio in Hawaii—

MARY: I've done the research.

FACE: —but it was the Babe who became Mister Hawk's protege and in our hearts, the biggest of the Little People.

MARY: What a jerk!

LARRY: Keep it down, Mo.

FACE: It was the Babe's endearing personality and talents as a performer that ensured her quickly becoming a featured artist—

MARY: You're trivializing her.

FACE: —and eventually led to her separate recording career. It was, of course, her now classic *Four*

Directions of Love, the first virtual reality disc released to the NorAmerican market that solidified her place in—

MARY: Look. Look again!

(Enter CLARISSE*)*

FACE: —And here we have another member of the congregation!

CLARISSE: Where'd he go?

LARRY: Clarisse Chrisjohn, Jo.

(A heartbeat)

CLARISSE: *(to* MARY*)* Hey, sweetie, did you see the Hawk?

FACE: Please, Miss Chrisjohn?

CLARISSE: *(to* FACE*)* A rabbity little guy?

FACE: May we speak with you about Babe Fisher?

CLARISSE: So you're from the TV?

FACE: Yes. And we're live for the news, Miss Chrisjohn. Would you say a few words about what this means to the failing spirit of the space program?

CLARISSE: *(playing to the camera)* Halleluiah! Be ye not afraid. I was low, yes, I was low, I was lost in the valley of death. But God is a great God. He works his ways with mystery upon mystery—

LARRY: Jo says we've got thirty seconds, Fred.

(A passing car beeps its horn)

CLARISSE: —with blessing upon blessing. She that was dead is alive again in our hearts today, we that were bereft only moments ago—

FACE: Thank you so much for your thoughts on this sad occasion.

CLARISSE: —now know joy once more, the world where the sun went down into the underworld, is born again with the dawn—

FACE: This is Fred Face, outside the Fisher Entertainment Community Centre on the New Nations Reserve, returning you to the studio.

(The FACE *image on the monitor is replaced by the silent but continuing news broadcast from the studio)*

MARY: You're such a pro, Freddy.

LARRY: We're clear.

FACE: I don't need these distractions!

CLARISSE: So, how'd I do?

FACE: Young woman, you're not authorized to be anywhere near this unit.

LARRY: *(turning off the monitor)* That was really real.

MARY: So, big deal, Fred.

CLARISSE: I'll take that as a complement.

FACE: You're under suspension.

CLARISSE: So where'd you say he went?

MARY: Everybody knows this is my story.

CLARISSE: Tommy Hawk?

LARRY: That was his cab that went by.

CLARISSE: That little bugger.

FACE: This story's too important for amateur hour.

MARY: Oh, take a break, Fred.

FACE: Larry! Have Jo bring me whatever she's got on Thomas Hawk. I'll be in the van. Call me for the update.

LARRY: Gotcha.

FACE: And get rid of your girlfriend. *(exits)*

CLARISSE: Hey, I know your face from someplace.

LARRY: I used to work *Moccasins on the Water.*

CLARISSE: When I used to testify? With the Raccoon in the choir!

MARY: You never told me.

CLARISSE: Fairy Larry?

LARRY: I was a transvestite for Christ!

CLARISSE: Fuck. Divine even in a surplus surplice, right? Hey, I got to go. There's this wake, sort of, over to her Grandma's suite at the hotel. I promised I'd mix them up some dips. Come on over after you're done here. *(moving on)*

MARY: Miss Chrisjohn!

LARRY: Hey, leave the poor woman alone. Okay?

MARY: This is my story. And you, you had an in on it all along and never told me.

LARRY: Hey, little miss, it was right there in my c.v. *(he exits)*

MARY: Miss Chrisjohn!

CLARISSE: Hiya, kid.

MARY: Please wait.

CLARISSE: What can I do you for?

MARY: Can I ask you some questions?

CLARISSE: *(moving on)* You a friend of Larry's? Come on then.

(Enter the mourning BARBARA *Buck and* MARTHA *Fisher, passing nearby,* MARTHA *supported and directed by her sister. A heartbeat)*

CLARISSE: We can do tea while I wash broccoli.

MARY: *(following)* You knew her, didn't you?

CLARISSE: Hey, when the sky falls, we're all a little chicken.

MARY: I'm sorry?

CLARISSE: You ain't the only one.

(A heartbeat)

MARY: I don't know what to say.

CLARISSE: Hey, kid, I thought you was a reporter.

(Exeunt BARBARA *and* MARTHA*)*

MARY: I am.

CLARISSE: This is it, home sweet dump.

MARY: We were there.

(The drum heartbeats again and the lights pulse)

CLARISSE: What is it? You okay?

MARY: At the Space Centre? We were there, you know, when it happened.

CLARISSE: You must have freaked. Hey, come on now.

MARY: I don't know what's wrong with me.

(A heartbeat and the lights dip and then CLARISSE *is in another light, sitting in one of two chairs, serving tea from a table)*

CLARISSE: You ought to eat something.

MARY: I don't know what's wrong with me.

CLARISSE: Come on. Cry if you want. Nothing wrong with that.

(Another heartbeat and the lights dip and then MARY *is also in the light with the chairs, sitting beside* CLARISSE*)*

CLARISSE: Some tea? You hungry?

MARY: I'm on a diet.

CLARISSE: You okay now? I been balling off and on myself the last couple days.

MARY: I was one of The Little People once. I met her.

CLARISSE: I don't think they hired white kids back then. Seems to me they would have lost their funding.

MARY: No, I mean I used to imagine it. That we were friends.

CLARISSE: Here. I only got the one spoon. I heard weirder fantasies in my career.

MARY: I want to know about her. The real her.

CLARISSE: It's spilt milk, kiddo. You want sugar?

MARY: No. Thank you. I'm on a diet.

CLARISSE: You okay now? I been balling off and on myself the last couple days.

(A heartbeat and the rock face pulses in and out)

MARY: My research says you were there when she was born.

CLARISSE: Ya. Like it says in the glossy magazines. 'Twas the night before Christmas and all through the house it was nuts.

MARY: The little log cabin by the river?

CLARISSE: Right. *(moving into the light from the window)* You can see the place from here when the leaves go.

MARY: I have a press release here somewhere.

CLARISSE: I know the story.

MARY: The Buck Agency. Native management for Native stars. Was he here today?

CLARISSE: Hey, the Buckaroo wouldn't have missed it. I mean she was his goddaughter.

MARY: Do you think he'd talk to me?

CLARISSE: Bet on it.

MARY: It says you grew up in the city.

(A heartbeat. The night city surrounds CLARISSE*)*

CLARISSE: I lived in town. Her mother and I palled around there.

MARY: So, this was back when she was a street worker?

CLARISSE: We headed home when her time came.

MARY: You have a social work degree too?

CLARISSE: I paid my dues. Working the street.

MARY: The situation of Native people in this country was shameful.

CLARISSE: It's all our own fault. Bad immigration laws.

MARY: I'm sorry?

CLARISSE: You ain't the only one. Hey, kid, it's a joke. An old one.

MARY: How can you make jokes?

CLARISSE: Maybe you'd call it faith. Fuck, I even went to midnight mass that Christmas.

MARY: There's a church out here?

CLARISSE: I mean after that cab come took her mom away. I been balling off and on myself the last couple days.

(A heartbeat and the night city fades)

MARY: You had taxis out here then?

CLARISSE: It ain't the bush! And that ain't the point. The point is there was one of them little mangers there in that church. And all of a sudden I saw her in it, little and bloody. And it was like I could hear her crying her first cry again. Saw her little mouth opening.

MARY: And you saw she was beautiful?

CLARISSE: I saw she was pitiful. A little girl. Like some hungry baby bird. It made me feel lonesome.

MARY: That's why you started helping street people?

CLARISSE: The situation of Native people in this country was shameful'? Look. This is what happened to me, okay?

MARY: I was hoping you'd tell me about her. You know, what was she like as a child? Okay? You did know her?

CLARISSE: Holy shit! You got the fucking press release! Can't you read? Let the Buckaroo give you the poop. Go on. Go. You can catch him before he leaves. He'll still be at the wake.

*(*MARY *gets up to go and then, as the drum begins to heartbeat, hesitates)*

MARY: I'm sorry, but I really need to know about her. I'm sorry. *(exits)*

CLARISSE: Social worker? No, that's Jack's story. Maybe I needed one way back when. After I saw how that baby looked. How useless.

(The night city pulses in slowly)

CLARISSE: I was on them streets again. I wasn't no hooker. Shit was I past that! I bet I looked as sad as I felt. Not what you'd call marketable. I just drank. Another indigenous tradition. I guess I was one of them folks they sweep under the rug when there's a party in town. And lucky me, they finally got the fucking Olympics that year. Cops scooped a whole bunch of us out of town and dumped us on the closest reserve. I mean, I grew up in the city. I'd never even been to no reserve before. I mean, holy! I was kind of scared of Indians then and all there was there was Indians everywhere. So, I started walking back to town. This was a ways up north of here. Rocks and trees, rocks and trees—trees and rocks. And no point thumbing, the way I looked. So, I was wandering up this side road that night as the sun went, looking for some place to crash, and I come upon these boarded-up buildings out there in the bush. I don't know how I got there. And one of them looked real weird, like big as a hangar for a plane, but all them walls was see-through, dirty, broken glass. I couldn't figure it. But it was getting cold and inside there was all these leaves and stuff and I thought I could build up a fire. And a bed. But then I wasn't tired no more.

(The night city fades and the petroglyphs pulse in)

CLARISSE: Under all that grass and leaves and stuff was a rock. And I could see that its face, even in the dark then, was a mess of cracks and holes and all these like drawings, cut right into it, animals and spirits, I guess. Like it looked alive and I remember I wondered if it hurt to get marked up like that, like you're tender after a tattoo, and if it was like holding its breath or maybe was just moving slow so I couldn't tell for sure in them shadows. Like them cracks was opening up like mouths.

(The petroglyphs fade and the Milky Way pulses in)

CLARISSE: Like the mouth of that baby. I was just lying there all night long, hearing water running under that ground, grumbling a hungry belly.

(The constellations in the star field flare even brighter on a beat, then they and CLARISSE*'s spot go to dark as the heartbeat stops)*

ACT ONE, SCENE THREE

(And again out of the dark and the heartbeating drum comes the pulsing night city where JACK *stands in the half-light. The heartbeat stops)*

JACK: But shit, then the Babe's face was there at the window and all them guys gone. And then it was the sun at that window.

(Then a monitor lights up and he turns toward its silent image of MARY *dancing and talking, introducing her virtuo show. The glow from the screen shows the real* MARY *waiting in one of two armchairs. A heartbeat and the night city fades as lights come up, autumn dusk in the grand hotel lobby, on* MARY. JACK *enters)*

JACK: Hiya, Mary. How's the dancing v.j. today?

MARY: I'm sorry?

JACK: Jack Buck. The Buck Agency? I recognized you from the virtuo show. I love that stuff. I turn it up loud and get right in there and do it with you. So, I hear you been hot on my trail.

MARY: Can you help me? I'm doing this story on—

JACK: The Babe! Hey, who isn't? I got interviews lined up from here to my heinie.

MARY: Maybe a personal perspective. As her uncle as well as her agent?

JACK: Ya, I took care of the Babe. So, what do you have in mind?

MARY: Well, I keep thinking of her, waving goodbye. When she was getting on the elevator to the Crazy Horse? The way she turns and...

JACK: Hey, don't sweat it, sweetheart.

MARY: I'm sorry. I don't know what's wrong.

JACK: Hey, why not cry? It's a heartbreaker picture, right? Her looking out at that camera? The clip everybody's been using? Great, ya? I taught her that myself. Ya, I said, Look, kiddo. It's part of the job. You got to be responsible, you want to be out there fronting for your people. You be open to the public. Heck, she was like six. This the sort of stuff you want?

MARY: That's so—professional.

JACK: I like you too, kiddo. That red really sets off your mouth.

MARY: Thank you.

JACK: What is it? Fire engine? When they told me you was here in the Arms, I thought, now that's the way I like it. That's how the truth about our Baby goes out to the kids.

MARY: But what do you feel about her?

JACK: So, here's your press kit.

MARY: She was more than a symbol to you.

JACK: It's got her bio, a bunch of eight by tens—they're all on disc in black-and-white and/or colour. It's got all the high points. Dig if you will this one.

MARY: Sitting in front of a helicopter.

JACK: Her very own whirlybird. Don't she looked cute in that jumpsuit. Indian red.

MARY: The way she's waving—this is the same pose.

JACK: Goodbye number three. She always did do that one best. The ones of her were on the front pages the day of the launch, we ain't got none of them yet. Her wearing the flight suit, holding her feather? Goodbye number four, especially Indian. I can courier you some over, though. Same address as on the show?

MARY: This is amazing to me.

JACK: Thanks. But the bio's updated. Quotes out of yesterday's service, including letters from the President, the P.M. and what's his big cheese face at the U.N.? That's the one I like.

MARY: You really took care of her, didn't you?

JACK: For my Baby, anything. That U.N. guy? He's planning on naming his next child Babe!

MARY: You're joking.

JACK: But at least he's got more smarts than them Toward Utopia dopes. Like this is no time to be New Age, this is a time for action.

MARY: Can't you tell me more about her?

JACK: Those stooges, they're holding seances, for fuck's sake. The message Babe brought has got to be kept alive in the world.

MARY: You don't cry, do you?

JACK: What?

MARY: I want to know the truth about her.

JACK: What are you talking about?

MARY: The real her.

JACK: But the truth's bigger than that.

MARY: I want to know the real person.

(On the monitor the virtuo show is interrupted and Fred FACE *appears, reporting, in front of images of the* Babe, *the shuttle launch, and the planet from orbit)*

JACK: This Native land. The four directions of love. That's her message. That's what you're here to sell the people on. You're here to keep Babe alive and out there.

MARY: You're hiding something about her.

JACK: Hey, look, something's going on. *(turns up the volume)*

FACE: —announced that the effort to retrieve the bodies of the crew of the Crazy Horse has been further delayed. It was relatives of the dearly departed Babe Fisher, contacted through the New Nations Media Centre, who expressed the greatest disappointment.

(Cut to CLARISSE *almost crowding* BARBARA *out of the shot)*

CLARISSE: So, how we supposed to put the Babe to rest? Can you tell me that?

JACK: That crazy bitch.

BARBARA: We're very disappointed.

CLARISSE: So, what the hell can you tell me? This is a bloody sacrilege.

JACK: Who the fuck let her in there!

(Back to Fred FACE *reporting)*

FACE: Scientists and programmers at the Kennedy Space Centre have brought some stability to the Crazy Horse orbit by a sequenced firing of its manoeuvring rockets but it is now reported that the shuttle has begun to spin on it longitudinal axis.

(Cut away to the shuttle in orbit, slowly turning)

FACE: A spokeswoman from the Space Centre was at a loss for an explanation of the cause. She also refused speculation regarding other experiments which may have been on board.

(A slow zoom in to the window of the turning shuttle where there is the suggestion of a face. A heartbeat)

FACE: The recovery shuttle has gone into a parking orbit until the spin of the Crazy Horse can be brought to a stop. The spin, however, appears to be accelerating. More news later.

(The image of MARY*'s face from her virtuo show cuts back in)*

JACK: *(turning the volume down)* Did you see that? The face?

MARY: That's my face.

JACK: No, there was a face in the fucking window. On the Crazy Horse. It's Babe.

(A heartbeat and a pulse of the Milky Way)

MARY: Mister Buck, she's dead.

JACK: She was looking out at us.

MARY: They're all dead. Okay? And they're all strapped in their seats. No one's alive up there.

JACK: Nobody believes in ghosts.

(A heartbeat and a pulse of the night city)

MARY: Mister Buck, are you okay?

JACK: You want personal stuff? Well, if somebody could haunt anybody, that kid could do me. Even as a baby—

MARY: Go on, Mister Buck.

JACK: Jack.

MARY: Okay.

JACK: Nice to talk first names, eh, Mary?

MARY: Go on, Jack.

JACK: You kind of remind me of her.

MARY: You said 'even as a baby?'

JACK: Babsy called her a wise child. Dark-eyed and watching and—do you got any tobacco? I need a smoke all of a sudden. Thanks. Gave it up long ago but—How old are you?

MARY: Twenty-five.

JACK: You make me feel ancient. But you're almost the same age.

MARY: As—Babe?

JACK: She always looked that way, sort of. Pressed up against the glass, trying to get in.

MARY: Trying to get in where?

JACK: The candy store, the world. Ya, like that.

MARY: Mister Buck—

JACK: Jack. Please. You got it, you got the look right now.

MARY: Look, Jack, I—

JACK: I really do like the way you dance.

(A heartbeat and a pulse of the Milky Way)

MARY: Mister Buck, maybe I better come back later—

JACK: Look, I'm old enough to be your—elder. You know what that means? It's like you got to listen to me when I want to talk. Hey, I'm making a funny. You ever hear tell of Curly Bear?

MARY: The medicine man on *Earth Tones*?

JACK: Ya, you all watch my programming. Curly's a pal of mine. An auto mechanic once upon a time. B.C., he says. Before computers. Ya, that's how old we are. To make extra cash he started this little dance group. Hell, what an eye for talent. Before long, he had a good little business going, being a fucking professional Indian. There's a poster.

MARY: Here's her name.

JACK: He asked me to help. All these folks asking him to do tours to the E.E.C. but him not able to handle the contracts and stuff. He said he couldn't read.

MARY: This is when he got you out of real estate?

JACK: He just told me what they was offering. I said sure. Sounds like easy money to me. Show business. Figured I could back a few plays, too. Keep the little woman entertained. Hell, he even tried to teach me some of them dances. One like this? *(he awkwardly dances a few steps)* I didn't know he was into the medicine then. I mean fuck, we sealed our partnership with my favourite scotch.

(BEAR *enters with a bottle of wine)*

BEAR: Hey, you want I should top you up there? Come on, Jack, when you going to get a chance again to sample the genuine European vintage?

JACK: Curly fucking loved the Babe.

BEAR: *(of* MARY *as if she were* BABE*)* How's the Barbarian doing?

JACK: Let her sleep, Curly.

(The night city slowly fades in, leaving MARY *in its shadows)*

BEAR: She'll get over the time lag quick. She's young. Wonder what she's dreaming about?

JACK: He's the one saw the dancer in her. That's how I ended up on his tour of the continent, looking after her.

BEAR: What a look on her face, eh?

JACK: The first time I ever really saw that look. Her asleep.

BEAR: Come on, Jack, let's go let her dream. Clarisse'll check on her.

JACK: That crazy fuck's not looking after—

BEAR: Hey! She's not your woman.

JACK: So, I shut up.

BEAR: We're in the middle of the Old World.

JACK: Some Belgian burg near where the German border used to be.

BEAR: We're here to paint it red. It's our duty. We'll repossess our souls from the churches and really impress the frauleins.

JACK: We didn't impressed nobody.

BEAR: We brave aboriginals must discover and take possession of the local brew.

JACK: We'd been in some church that day. Old as Rome, so they said. It was all dug up, a holy mess. And they had these bones, were on show, under glass.

BEAR: How would you like it if somebody pulled your covers off? How they supposed to rest in peace?

JACK: Some guy from a couple of thousand years back. Some priest, they thought.

BEAR: But they don't know. They don't know for sure.

JACK: Curly got all weird about it. He said it showed disrespect.

BEAR: It's none of their fucking business. Poking their noses in where they don't belong all the fucking time.

JACK: That's what got him started drinking so crazy. We ended up stumbling around them streets in the middle of the fucking night.

BEAR: See how they like it. We'll invade their privacy.

JACK: Like he decided we'd break into that castle there, this, I guess, museum in the middle of the place.

BEAR: See how their dead like it.

JACK: All's I remember is steps and steps going up this mountain.

BEAR: Come on, Jack. I can see the gate.

JACK: Shit, Curly, I'm dying here.

BEAR: Come on. Upsy-daisy. Or are you yellow? It'll make a man of you.

JACK: I don't know how we got over the wall.

BEAR: A white man. *(he disappears in the shadows)*

(The drum begins the dreamy heartbeat)

JACK: And the bugger disappears on me. Hello? Curly? Bear, you idiot! I was alone on top of this fucking high castle wall in the middle of the night. I tell you, you sober up quick. Curly? Why was I whispering? I heard voices. Down below me, in the castle's yard, a light. Must be what? Guards. The night shift. Shit, I'll just tell them I'm lost.

(The night city begins to pulse with the beat)

JACK: Hey, us Canadians must do it all the time. I mean it was a long way, more than a couple storeys down, once I found them stairs, feeling along the stone walls. And shit, going across that yard, I kept tripping over stuff in the grass. I could hear them laughing in whatever language it was through that window. That's where Curly had got to. I looked in and there he was. Tied to a fucking chair. With this circle of guys in white coats around him, poking him, pinching his skin, looking at his teeth and just laughing away. And he was laughing along with them. Till one of them started slipping this blade round the edge of his hair. Taking his scalp. Shit, he mewled like a cat under a boot.

(MARY *comes out of the shadows)*

JACK: And I just knew his hair would go on display there. And mine would too if I let them know for sure where I was from. I wanted out. But I fell. My hand got a hold of something slimy I lifted up into the light from the window. A bone. A human fucking bone from this part of an arm! That fucking yard was full of them. Bones, and teeth and hair. And there I was, me and that bugger Curly Bear, looking up at them laughing, looking up out of a glass display case.

MARY: Mister Buck? Jack?

JACK: But shit, then the Babe's face was there at the window and all them guys gone. Just her face with that look. And then it was the sun at that window.

(The heartbeat and the night city fade)

MARY: Are you okay?

JACK: And Curly was outside the gate. Sleeping on a bench. Innocent as all fuck. I knew the fucker'd done a number on me but...

MARY: What was it?

JACK: That place? All them bones that don't rest in peace. And I just knew I had to bring Babe home.

MARY: Oh, you care about her, even in your dreams.

JACK: I knew Babe needed to know just where her home was. And I made sure she did her dancing here.

MARY: You took care of her.

JACK: No, kiddo, she took care of me. And that wasn't no dream.

MARY: 'For my Baby, anything.'

JACK: I miss her so much, Mary. I miss her so much.

(She embraces him and then they kiss. A heartbeat and a pulse of Milky Way and then blackout)

ACT ONE, SCENE FOUR

(A heartbeat and the path through the clearing appears. Then a monitor comes on, silently rerunning the news about the delayed recovery mission. The glow shows MARY *asleep in bed and* BARBARA *standing beside her, gazing in the direction of the path)*

BARBARA: She told me that little man lived there. She said he was hiding there in the grove. You know what? I believed her. I believed her.

(A heartbeat and the path fades and morning lights come up in the hotel bedroom. BARBARA *turns the monitor off and then sits down on the bed)*

BARBARA: Excuse me, dear, don't get up.

MARY: *(waking)* What?

BARBARA: Don't get up, but did he leave? Did Jack leave?

MARY: Who are—How did you—?

BARBARA: I'm Barbara. I just wanted to talk—

MARY: You're his wife!

BARBARA: —to him about the will, when we'll be reading it. Excuse me. What did you say?

MARY: You're his wife.

BARBARA: Martha, my sister, she runs the hotel, she lives just upstairs—

MARY: You're Barbara Buck!

BARBARA: —and she gave me the key so I could surprise him? Oh, I used to be his wife, so don't you worry your head, I know you're one of his little television friends.

MARY: One of his little friends?

BARBARA: You are an adult, aren't you? Legally? Sometimes he lacks common sense.

MARY: Of course I'm an adult.

BARBARA: Once I would have said common decency.

MARY: I'm Mary Oh,. I do the number one V.R. show.

BARBARA: But now I know how it is, 'there at the top', as he says.

MARY: What time is it?

BARBARA: I do miss him too sometimes—excuse me? Oh, it's almost lunch time, have you eaten?

MARY: Look, he left a couple of hours ago.

BARBARA: Back to what he calls 'lala land'?

MARY: I should get dressed, okay?

BARBARA: Oh, no, don't get up, dear. I'll let you go back to sleep. I guess I'll just have to call him at that studio, I don't like using that video link-up. I always feel like I need make up and who has the time anymore with everything the way it is?

(A heartbeat)

MARY: You said 'reading a will?' You knew the Babe too?

BARBARA: Of course I did, dear, she was my grandniece. You are a sleepy head.

MARY: But why a will?

BARBARA: I would like to talk to you about her but I think that's Jack's business?

MARY: She was young.

BARBARA: That's what he always says.

MARY: I need a story with a more personal spin.

BARBARA: A story?

MARY: I'm reporting on this for my show.

BARBARA: You've been crying too, haven't you? I can hear it in your voice.

(A heartbeat)

MARY: Young people really admired her. Please?

BARBARA: I suppose it would be all right, I'd like to, what harm can it do?

MARY: Jack—Mister Buck—he told me about—

BARBARA: No more harm can be done now.

MARY: —about taking her to Europe to dance.

BARBARA: I can hear it in your voice.

MARY: I should get dressed, okay?

BARBARA: Oh, no, don't get up. I'll let you go back to sleep.

(A heartbeat and the lights do down and the monitor comes back on, silently rerunning the news about the delayed recovery mission and the glow shows MARY *still asleep in bed and* BARBARA *standing beside her)*

BARBARA: You look almost like her. Except you're so pale.

MARY: *(waking)* What?

BARBARA: We couldn't have our own children. It was too—

MARY: Who are—How did you—?

BARBARA: We always thought of her as almost ours, you know? You do look almost like her.

MARY: I look almost like her?

BARBARA: He was so glad to get home. Children are magic, he said. He really loved her, yes, he got her a yellow dress.

MARY: She wore a lot of yellow?

BARBARA: Yes, he got her a yellow dress. Do you have a yellow dress?

(A heartbeat and the morning lights come back up and the monitor is dark and BARBARA *is sitting on* MARY*'s bed)*

BARBARA: After that trip Jack didn't care if he ever saw another church again in his life. You know how he talks? He sure upset Martha. There's no call for that kind of language, she said. I set up the halfway house myself. It used to be our own house.

MARY: So, was that the Babe's idea? She did all that work with street kids.

BARBARA: Nobody was taking care of them.

MARY: And Babe gave you money to do that?

BARBARA: The house Jack bought. People are always talking about the future but all they care about is now. Once she had money, well what else is it good for? That's what she said.

MARY: That's where the Little People idea came from?

BARBARA: Our children, some of them, they're so talented.

MARY: So, she inspired Mister Buck to create the show?

BARBARA: I don't know, dear, maybe I should talk with Jack first?

MARY: It's okay. Jack's already talked with me.

BARBARA: Jack's already talked with you?

MARY: Please?

BARBARA: You check with him before you print anything—he's so careful about her.

MARY: Of course I will.

BARBARA: Well, then, ask away.

MARY: Tell me about her mother.

BARBARA: Well, Martha, my sister, she was kind of upset because Lena wasn't married, Martha's very Christian.

MARY: Lena? Who's Lena?

BARBARA: I didn't want her growing up with that over her head either and Jack said it would be better this way. Lena was Babe's mother.

MARY: But wait. That's not right. Boo Fisher was.

BARBARA: Lena did ask Boo to take care of her baby. I guess she knew somehow she was dying.

MARY: Her mother? But it was her father who died. An accident building a bridge.

BARBARA: We don't know who her father was.

MARY: But that's not what I read. I read he was a steel worker—

BARBARA: Maybe I should check with Jack before—

MARY: Wait a minute here. You've been lying to me. What's going on? Boo was her mother and—

BARBARA: I don't think I should say anything more. I can't tell what you want.

(A heartbeat)

MARY: You people are so two-faced.

BARBARA: I can't tell you what you want.

MARY: I just want to get her story.

BARBARA: What do you want? What do you want?

MARY: I'm sorry.

BARBARA: I need to talk to Jack!

MARY: Missus Buck, I'm sorry. I didn't mean to upset you.

BARBARA: That's his business. I can't tell.

MARY: Tell me what you want to tell me. Please.

BARBARA: I can't.

MARY: Anything.

BARBARA: You've been crying, haven't you?

MARY: Okay?

BARBARA: I can hear it in your voice.

(A heartbeat and the path fades in)

BARBARA: We had her with us, Jack and me, on our trip out west.

*(*JACK *enters and sits in front of* MARY, *turning the bed into a car.* BARBARA *moves into it too)*

BARBARA: I was always wanting to go there, I wanted to see totem poles. It was sort of our second honey moon.

JACK: Let's take the kid with us. Give the old Fish a break.

BARBARA: Well, he thought Martha did all the work, taking care of her, he just didn't trust Boo to do her bit of anything. So, we drove across Vancouver Island.

JACK: This road is the shits.

BARBARA: You know him, can you imagine how he drives? And I was so afraid we were lost. But then Babe spoke up.

MARY as BABE: Uncle! Uncle, look!

JACK: What is it, darling?

BARBARA: That sign, Jack, see.

JACK: 'Cathedral Grove?'

BARBARA: I wonder if maybe there's a chapel there. Can we stop?

JACK: Come on, Babsy, I thought you wanted to go see the whales. The catamaran won't wait.

MARY as BABE: Please, Uncle, I know this place. It's beautiful.

BARBARA: And it was. We pulled into the parking lot and got out and it was just so cool and smelled like cedars or pine freshener? We could hear a few little birds, and way, way up in the trees where the sun was, the wind was...

(A heartbeat)

JACK: They're swaying like drunks.

BARBARA: It's like they're alive.

MARY as BABE: They are alive, Auntie.

BARBARA: I know, Babe. I just meant—

MARY as BABE: They're talking to each other.

BARBARA: It's funny. Babe and I were whispering.

JACK: Think of all the board feet you could get out of that baby.

BARBARA: Jack, the sign says these trees are protected, they're among the oldest living things in the world.

JACK: They're not doing nobody any good just standing here, Babsy.

BARBARA: They're making me feel good, Jack.

JACK: Hey, Babs, your Big Buck can do that for you.

BARBARA: Oh, Jack, don't. Not in front of—

(A heartbeat)

JACK: Where is she?

BARBARA: She was right there.

MARY: Where is she?

JACK: Babe! Babe! Answer me!

MARY: Where was she?

BARBARA: Gone. Just gone. We looked all over that place for her for it seemed like hours. What will Martha say, Jack?

(The path fades down)

JACK: I'm going to go call the cops.

BARBARA: But Jack, you can't leave me here.

JACK: If you knew how to drive, you could go. You'll be all right. There might be an emergency phone at that last camp site we passed. Look, Babsy, I'll be back quick. You got to keep on looking.

BARBARA: It'll be dark soon, Jack.

JACK: What will Martha say, Babsy? (exiting)

BARBARA: And he left me there. Just left me there.

MARY: Were you angry? Where was she?

(The Milky Way slowly replaces the path)

BARBARA: I don't know. I just kept walking around, kind of looking. It's not really that big a place, the grove, but they're big, those redwoods, like buildings, but there aren't so many of them. I noticed these pretty little flowers glowing, yellow, close to the roots. And then it was dark.

MARY: Were you frightened?

BARBARA: Well, I just couldn't believe he'd leave me like that, but that place, I guess it was better than being in church. I didn't miss him at all.

MARY: But what about Babe?

BARBARA: She came back, just wandered out of the woods. There was nothing wrong with her.

MARY as BABE: How long's Uncle Jack gonna be gone? I'm hungry.

BARBARA: Then Jack came back with a couple of big forest rangers on his heels.

(JACK and the TWO RANGERS enter)

BARBARA: And when he saw her there, he looked so embarrassed.

JACK: Where the—have you been?

BARBARA: Jack, please—

JACK: Do you know what time it is? Do you know how worried we were?

MARY
as BABE: I'm sorry, Uncle. I was just over there. Talking with that Little Man.

JACK: What little man?

MARY
as BABE: He lives in that tree.

(The TWO RANGERS *exchange a look and shrug in unison)*

JACK: Don't give me that crap. I won't stand for it.

MARY
as BABE: But he knew my name. He knew who I was.

JACK: Crazy kid.

(In unison, the TWO RANGERS *look at* JACK, *exchange a look, about-face and exit)*

MARY
as BABE: Really, Auntie, he knew all about me.

BARBARA: Tell me later, sweetie.

JACK: Get in the car. What did I do to deserve this?

(The Milky Way fades)

BARBARA: And Martha was so mad. Maybe if we hadn't told her, Jack. She wouldn't talk to him.

JACK: I kind of like the quiet.

(The morning light returns)

MARY: But what about her?

BARBARA: She told me all about that little man that lived there? She said he was hiding out there. In the grove? She said he was dressed in leather, and he spoke Indian. But she could understand what he said. You know what? *(she embraces* MARY*)* I believed her. I believed her and I wished I'd seen him too. But then they say the Little People don't like grown ups.

(A heartbeat. JACK *kisses* BARBARA *goodbye and then exits without looking back)*

BARBARA: It was just about a year later I left Jack. I guess I just knew I needed to do this, to look after a lot of kids, especially since we couldn't have any of our own— And I always tell them all I know about the Little People, even when they think I'm being silly. I even tell the white kids. You live here, too. Jack always said— But I thought he wouldn't be happy if we adopted. His brothers and sister, they'd been in a residential school that had burned down. He's the last one of his family. He still cries for them, you know?

(Blackout)

ACT ONE, SCENE FIVE

(In darkness, the dreamy heartbeating drum. On a beat the night city pulses in around MARY *who mimes a section of the report she did at the launch to a camera in the shadows. On another heartbeat, a monitor comes on running her image from the launch with the sound on at a murmur. The glow from the monitor reveals* MARTHA *sitting at a desk, watching the screen. On another beat the night city and* MARY *fade while a spot of late afternoon light comes up on* MARTHA, *in mourning. A final heartbeat and the monitor cuts to a spreadsheet and* MARTHA *begins working)*

MARTHA: Eight and three makes eleven. And fifteen is twenty-six. And you carry the two. And two and eight makes ten. And six—who's there? Someone there? No. Where am I? Ten? And six makes sixteen and then carry the one. Save total. Six hundred and sixty—save me, please heaven. *(she suddenly picks up the telephone)* Hello? Hello? No one there. *(she gets to her feet, paces the room, begins to hum and then to sing Swing Low, Sweet Chariot)* ...coming for to carry me home. Swing low, sweet chariot, Coming for to carry me home. I looked over yonder and what—Who's there? Someone there?

(A heartbeat and a spot reveals MARY*)*

MARY: Missus Fisher?

(A heartbeat and a spot reveals the ANGEL*)*

ANGEL: You Martha? Martha Fisher?

(A heartbeat and a spot reveals RICKY *holding a baby-sized bundle)*

RICKY: Hey, Lady. Lady!

MARTHA: Oh, yes. Yes, who is it?

MARY: Hello, I'm Mary Oh.

MARTHA: Mary?

RICKY: Lady, it's about this here baby.

MARTHA: I don't know no Mary.

ANGEL: I've got the news for you, great big news to fill the house.

MARY: I'm from the news.

MARTHA: You have news? News about Babe?

MARY: No, Missus Fisher, I left a message on your machine.

RICKY: You know what they want to do to this kid?

MARTHA: I don't know what to think.

ANGEL: I got you tidings of great big joy. Great big joy!

MARY: I'm doing a story about her.

MARTHA: It's taking so long.

RICKY: Hush, little Babe, enough water works.

MARY: Well, they're sending up another shuttle in the morning.

ANGEL: Great big joy to fill your house!

MARTHA: But patience is a virtue.

MARY: They think they know why the Crazy Horse is spinning like that.

MARTHA: Our virtue will be rewarded.

RICKY: Don't you worry about this here kid.

ANGEL: Do you hear me?

MARY: Will you talk with me about her? About Babe?

MARTHA: I was doing accounts.

RICKY: The buggers won't get no hold on her. No sir.

MARY: I can't seem to get the story straight.

MARTHA: You always have to keep busy.

MARY: I mean I just want to know the truth.

MARTHA: Look at the numbers. Eight and three makes eleven. And fifteen is twenty-six. Six hundred and —it's all in the black. It all makes sense.

ANGEL: Do you hear the news?

MARTHA: Like the numbers of hymns on a Sunday.

ANGEL: *(sings softly while the dialogue continues)*
Jesus will be here,
In my Father's house.
Jesus will be here,
In my Father's house.
Jesus will be here,
In my Father's house.
And there'll be joy,
Joy, sweet joy.

MARY: Missus Fisher?

MARTHA: I'm sorry?

MARY: It's me. Mary.

RICKY: Hey, Lady. Lady!

MARTHA: Call me Granma.

MARY: Missus Fisher, I'm not your granddaughter.

RICKY: Hey, Granma, they think they can buy this kid.

MARTHA: I can't stop thinking about her.

MARY: Everybody's thinking about her right now.

MARTHA: Everybody calls me Granma. The desk clerk and the Bingo callers call me Granma. Are you hungry?

MARY: The callers call you Granma?

RICKY: They act like they ain't got no relations.

MARTHA: There's leftover turkey in the fridge. Her favourite stuffing. Cranberry and sage.

MARY: But why do the callers call you Granma?

MARTHA: Isn't it nice and friendly? That man said it was good business. The man my sister married.

MARY: Jack Buck? Missus Fisher—Granma, please—

(A heartbeat and the night city pulses in and the ANGEL *stops singing and both she and* RICKY *turn to look at* MARY*)*

MARTHA: Granma Fisher's Bingo Palace. I felt such a fool. You know, he wanted to take the child. When she was first born. I don't know what he wanted with her. I don't know what gets into men. I think the blackness was in him then, the evil.

RICKY: *(to* MARY*)* We'll hole up here for a while?

MARTHA: They say that last time he tried to kill the child. But it was not for him to crucify you.

MARY: What are you talking about?

ANGEL: *(to* MARY*)* Do you hear me? Do you hear the news?

MARTHA: I knew you would come. Waiting was hard, but I knew.

MARY: Missus—Granma, please—

(A heartbeat and the ANGEL *guides* MARY *into* MARTHA*'s embrace and* MARY *becomes* BABE *on her lap)*

MARTHA: Come to me. Come on. Come to your Granma. Now you're going to listen to me.

RICKY: Hush, little baby, hush.

MARY
as BABE: Okay, Granma.

MARTHA: This is important. Do you hear? Nobody else knows. This is our secret?

ANGEL: Hey, I got the news for you. Great big joy to fill your house.

MARY
as BABE: Okay.

MARTHA: You were born on Christmas.

MARY
as BABE: Everybody knows that.

RICKY: Hush, little baby, hush.

MARTHA: Do you know what that means?

MARY
as BABE: One set of presents.

MARTHA: Don't be stupid.

MARY
as BABE: That's what Uncle Jack says.

MARTHA: That man! Listen to me. Now listen. And sit still.

MARY
as BABE: Your lap's too small.

MARTHA: Just be still, bony bum. An angel appeared to me.

MARY
as BABE: An angel?

ANGEL: Hey, I got the news for you.

MARTHA: To me. She appeared and said you was coming.

MARY
as BABE: Like an angel with wings? With a light around her head?

MARTHA: A halo.

ANGEL: The princess is coming. It's her time.

MARTHA: Yes, that's what she said. The princess is coming.

ANGEL: She's coming home to you tonight.

MARY
as BABE: The princess?

RICKY: This here baby.

MARTHA: It was you, Baby, you.

ANGEL: Are you ready?

MARY
as BABE: An Indian princess?

MARTHA: You're my Indian princess.

ANGEL: Are you ready for the joy?

ANGEL
and RICKY: *(sing softly together while the dialogue continues)*
Oh, she will be here,
In my Father's house.
Oh, she will be here,
In my Father's house.
Oh, she will be here,
In my Father's house.
And there'll be joy,
Joy, sweet joy.

MARY
as BABE: Granma, why are you crying?

MARTHA: You're God's love in the flesh.

MARY
as BABE: Please don't cry.

MARTHA: My patience has been rewarded. It's just like your grandfather, Leonard.

MARY
as BABE: What is it, Granma?

MARTHA: He came back to me. After he died. I was afraid you wouldn't come back. I have such little faith.

MARY
as BABE: I'll always come back.

MARTHA: When you were born, the animals saved you, took you out of that house of death, that city of blackness.

MARY
as BABE: It's all right, Granma.

MARTHA: The Raccoon crept into that dirty house and took you in his arms.

MARY
as BABE: You'll be safe here.

MARTHA: He took you off to where the Bear sleeps.

MARY
as BABE: You'll be safe.

MARTHA: Tell me about that place. You never told me before.

MARY
as BABE: I have to go.

MARTHA: You told Auntie Boo. Did you really say only the animals love us like that?

MARY
as BABE: I have to go away now, Granma. I have to go and die.

(On a heartbeat, the night city fades and the Milky Way pulses in and the singers stop and look at MARY *and* MARTHA*)*

MARTHA: No.

MARY: *(twisting out of* MARTHA*'s arms)* What? What?

MARTHA: It's not right. It's not your turn.

(The ANGEL *turns* MARY *to face* MARTHA. RICKY *moves to a distance)*

MARY: What did she say?

MARTHA: I should be the one. But you said 'I have to go die first. The raccoons and the bears? They're God's messengers.'

RICKY: I didn't say that.

MARY: That's crazy.

MARTHA: They told you to get ready. They told you. I didn't want to believe it.

MARY: But what about her life?

ANGEL: We didn't say that. Oh, you stupid!—

RICKY: Hush, little baby, hush.

MARTHA: It's what the angel said. It was time.

ANGEL: That's not the news. That's not it.

MARY: What about babies of her own?

RICKY: No. One day—

MARTHA: This is what you were born to do.

MARY: Why?

MARTHA: To die for our sins.

RICKY: Ya, one day—

MARY: Why do the children have to die?

MARTHA: Are you sure, Babe? Are you sure? Why can't I die for you?

RICKY: One day she'll take care of all of us.

MARTHA: And you laughed and said: Don't worry, Granma. I know what I'm doing. And here you are, back from the dead.

RICKY: That's the story?

MARY: Listen to me, you old fool.

RICKY: That's the truth?

MARY: Would she have carried a bomb?

ANGEL: I've got such news to fill the house.

MARTHA: Does the Bear sleep in Heaven?

ANGEL: With joy.

MARTHA: Tell me, Babe.

ANGEL: Joy?

MARTHA: Is it like how church used to be?

MARY: Why would she do this? Nothing I've ever heard—

MARTHA: Is your mother there? Your grandfather? I hope he's there. I know you never knew him.

MARY: Missus Fisher? Missus Fisher!

MARTHA: Does the Bear talk about hell? I don't like to think about that.

MARY: Look at me.

(The dream heartbeat begins)

MARTHA: The things of this world are a terrible weight. I'm only an old woman. You're so young. You're so pretty. I don't understand, Baby. Is the kingdom of heaven at hand? Praise God from whom all blessings—Look at me, Babe. Is it true? Is this the end of the world? Is that what the animals told you? You're so young, so pretty. You rose again from the dead. My baby, my dearest. Send your love among us. We are the weak ones. You are strong. The daughter of God. Oh, praise him.

Oh, she will be here,
In my Father's house.
Yes, she will be here,
In my Father's—

(she falls writhing, speaking in tongues)

MARY: Oh, sugar. Missus Fisher, are you all—? Can I help? Granma?

(The heartbeat stops)

MARTHA: Who's there?

RICKY: No, lady! No. *(his spot goes out)*

MARY: It's me.

ANGEL: Oh, why aren't you ready for the joy? *(her spot goes out)*

MARY: It's me, Mary?

MARTHA: Oh, you're the angel! *(she bursts into flame)*

MARY: *(scurrying for safety)* Oh, my God—

(The flames totally consume MARTHA*)*

MARY: What's going on? What's going on? What's going on? *(she faints)*

(A heartbeat and the flames die down as the night city lights flare. Then a blackout)

END OF ACT

KYOTOPOLIS

ACT TWO, SCENE ONE

(The dreamy heart for four beats. Then on the next heartbeat, a snow-filled monitor comes on. On the next beat, the night city pulses in to show BOO, *standing in the half-light, looking toward the monitor. On the following heartbeat, the night city and* BOO *fade. And then on a last beat the monitor blares on: Fred* FACE *is reporting. The monitor shows clips of the launch and disaster)*

FACE: —and it has now been confirmed that yesterday morning's mission of mercy to the Crazy Horse was not successful. It was because of the possibly delicate nature of such a recovery operation and in respect for the sensitivities of the families of the dead that the Agency had not allowed live coverage.

(The monitor shows stills and the same file clips of the spinning shuttle)

FACE: And it has now also been confirmed that efforts to take control of the onboard computers have also failed. It had been the hope of scientists that the sequenced firing of the main engines would bring to a stop the shuttle's still mysterious spinning.

(The monitor shows an animated image of the shuttle spinning like a top with the suggestion of a halo forming around it)

FACE: These unexplained difficulties in dealing with the spin phenomenon are being exacerbated by the strong magnetic field the spinning is unexpectedly generating. It is also feared that the increased acceleration in the spin could lead to destruction of the multi-billion-dollar space craft and the desecration of the remains of the deceased.

(The monitor shows the animation of the shuttle blowing apart in a spray of debris)

FACE: This could cause profound damage to the spirit of the space program.

(And we now take you to our man on the scene outside the Fisher Centre on the New Nations Reserve where the funeral of MARTHA *Fisher, grandmother of* BABE *Fisher, is now drawing to a close)*

(The monitor cuts to an image of LARRY *reporting)*

LARRY: Hiya, Fred. I'm here with Clarisse Chrisjohn, a friend of the Fisher family, who has agreed to speak with us on this sad occasion.

*(*CLARISSE *moves into the shot)*

LARRY: How you feeling today, Miss Chrisjohn?

CLARISSE: Hey, Larry, I'm not doing cartwheels. This is all real weird for us.

(Outdoor evening light up on LARRY *reporting,* CLARISSE, *and* JO *as the camera operator)*

LARRY: This was such a bizarre death. And so soon after the Crazy Horse.

CLARISSE: I was low, I was lost in the valley of death.

LARRY: Is there any sort of comment you can make about what happened?

CLARISSE: It's hard to handle it sometimes. But I know Martha Fisher had faith.

LARRY: They say cases of spontaneous combustion are pretty rare.

CLARISSE: I hope they're right.

LARRY: Well, they say there was someone with her.

CLARISSE: Our cops got the girl now.

LARRY: Do you know who it was?

CLARISSE: That friend of yours. That Mary Oh virtuo babe?

LARRY: Really?

CLARISSE: Seems the detective don't believe old women can burst into flame.

LARRY: I'll let you go now.

CLARISSE: Larry, God is a great God. He works his ways with mystery upon mystery. They're alive in our hearts.

LARRY: We've been talking with Clarisse Chrisjohn, a friend of the Fisher family.

CLARISSE: At least old Martha won't have to cry over the Babe no more.

LARRY: Thanks. We return now to the studio.

CLARISSE: No sweat. You're a good kid.

(The monitor goes dark)

CLARISSE: You didn't know.

LARRY: I just got this gig this morning.

CLARISSE: Well, that's good news.

LARRY: I should have guessed.

*(*MARY *enters)*

CLARISSE: Speak of the devil.

JO: What's she doing here?

CLARISSE: I'll see what's cooking. *(goes to* MARY*)*

LARRY: Pay attention. The cops think she was the one set the old lady on fire.

JO: No shit?

CLARISSE: Hey, I hear you've been getting up to no good. How you doing?

MARY: They wouldn't let me out.

JO: Thank you, God.

CLARISSE: Hey, you're out now.

MARY: I wanted to come to the service.

CLARISSE: Probably wouldn't have been a good idea.

MARY: I wanted to tell what happened.

CLARISSE: Lots of reporters here.

JO: Hiya, Mary! How you doing?

MARY: Jo?

CLARISSE: It's kind of even crazier than before. Hey, come on.

MARY: I don't know what's wrong with me.

CLARISSE: Cry if you want to.

(A heartbeat and the path fades in)

CLARISSE: This is a rough time for all of us.

MARY: They kept asking me all these questions.

CLARISSE: They want to know what happened.

JO: Hiya, Mary! How's tricks?

CLARISSE: They know you was a witness.

LARRY: Lay off, will you. You're making a fool of yourself.

MARY: But they wouldn't believe me.

JO: Hiya, hot stuff!

MARY: Could we go someplace else?

LARRY: Shut up. A woman died.

JO: On account of her.

CLARISSE: The wake's at Babsy's.

JO: My career's in the toilet because of Miss Oh.

LARRY: Your mouth belongs there too.

MARY: I wanted to explain.

JO: Well, fuck you. *(exits)*

MARY: It wasn't my fault.

(A heartbeat and the lights fade except for the path on which MARY *is left alone for a moment. Then another heartbeat and she and* CLARISSE *are inside and the path is gone)*

CLARISSE: Come on, sit down. I'll go see if Babsy wants to hear your story.

MARY: Mizz Chrisjohn, wait.

CLARISSE: Look. She needs to hear what happened. Martha was her sister. Okay? I'll see about something to eat too. I know what sort of crap that lock-up serves.

MARY: I don't know if I can now.

(A heartbeat and the lights fade. Then another heartbeat and the inside lights come back up and CLARISSE *is gone and* LARRY *enters and sits down beside* MARY*)*

LARRY: How's Miss Pale Face doing?

MARY: I feel like shit, okay?

LARRY: You look like it too.

MARY: Fuck off.

LARRY: It's not just a fashion statement now?

MARY: Don't talk to me.

LARRY: Lighten up, little miss.

*(*BARBARA *and* CLARISSE *enter)*

BARBARA: Remember how she always talked about seeing Leonard after he died? At the foot of her bed?

MARY: What's that smell?

CLARISSE: The old doll loved to tell that one.

LARRY: Sweetgrass.

CLARISSE: Like he seemed to show up more as a spook than he had in the flesh.

LARRY: Purification.

BARBARA: All last week she was talking about him, expecting to see Babe any minute.

MARY: There's something evil going on here, Larry.

CLARISSE: Like being dead doesn't affect your social life.

MARY: Look at them. They're all acting as if nothing has happened.

BARBARA: She wanted to believe that so much.

MARY: They're up to something inhuman.

LARRY: Hey, Mo. Look at me.

BARBARA: I've never seen a ghost.

LARRY: You're the one was there when it happened.

MARY: What the hell's that supposed to mean?

BARBARA: I'd be afraid to.

LARRY: You got a lot of nerve calling people names.

MARY: It's because I'm white, isn't it?

CLARISSE: Might be a nice change from flesh and blood.

LARRY: Little Miss Oh, why does it all have to do with you?

MARY: You people all stick together, don't you?

LARRY: Hey, Mo, I don't want to hear this evil crap.

BARBARA: Might be a nice change.

MARY: Where you going?

LARRY: I got forms to fill out. *(he exits)*

MARY: Larry!

BARBARA: Now I half expect to turn around and see Martha.

CLARISSE: Pale as her own spreadsheets. Here she is.

BARBARA: What? Oh, Jack's little friend.

CLARISSE: Jack knows her?

BARBARA: She was the one? With Martha? It was her?

CLARISSE: Wait a minute, Babs. She wants to tell you what—

BARBARA: Let him talk to her. *(she exits)*

CLARISSE: She's kind of upset. How you doing?

MARY: Oh, I shouldn't be here.

CLARISSE: You may be right. But sit tight.

(Enter JACK*)*

CLARISSE: Here's the eats. What is it?

MARY: You're so kind to me. *(she eats)*

(A heartbeat and the path appears and the LADY *in black enters along it and waves to* CLARISSE*)*

CLARISSE: It's just tea and banic. What I do for comfort food.

MARY: Who's that?

CLARISSE: What? Oh, for—Here eat up. *(she goes to the LADY)*

*(*JACK *comes and sits with* MARY*)*

JACK: Some party, eh?

CLARISSE: Who are you supposed to be?

LADY: Guess. *(strikes a* MARY *Oh v.j. pose)* Okay?

JACK: How's my dancing v.j.? She wasn't trying to convert you, was she?

CLARISSE: This is a wake.

LADY: But I'm wearing black.

(The LADY *rummages in her purse and a piece of paper falls out unnoticed)*

MARY: Who's that?

LADY: Look, look. Even the lipstick!

MARY: That woman talking to Mizz Chrisjohn.

CLARISSE: Have some respect, for fuck's sake.

JACK: Search me. Never seen the likes of her here before.

LADY: She liked the way I dress.

CLARISSE: Well, I don't!

(Enter BOO*)*

CLARISSE: You look like a whore.

LADY: The voice of experience.

(CLARISSE *pushes the* LADY *to exit in a hurry, and they run into* BOO *and take her off with them)*

JACK: She a reporter?

MARY: Dressed like that? You can't even see her face.

JACK: What do I know? Hey, I saw her gabbing with your pal a few minutes back.

MARY: With Larry? Maybe he'll tell me.

JACK: So, how are you?

MARY: I'm okay. You vouched for me.

JACK: The constable owed me one. Hey, I really do like you, Mare. *(he kisses her)*

MARY: Jack, I don't usually do that.

JACK: Kiss elders, you mean?

MARY: I mean, I hardly know you.

JACK: You mean, you do like me too?

(They kiss)

JACK: Hey, how'd you like to come work with me? I know they've dropped you off your virtuo show. It'd be great to have someone I can talk to to work with.

*(*BOO *enters again)*

MARY: I might go to jail.

*(*BOO *picks up the piece of paper the* LADY *in black lost)*

JACK: I got lawyers. Mare, nobody's going to convict you of tossing matches at old Martha.

MARY: How can you talk like that? Death isn't a joke.

*(*BOO *gets a laugh out of the paper)*

MARY: You're all acting like death isn't real. Do you think Babe has risen from the dead too?

JACK: What is it?

MARY: That's what Martha said, okay?

JACK: It's kind of hard to argue with fire, Mare.

BOO: Hey, Uncle! Uncle Jack. Auntie wants to talk to you. I said Auntie—

JACK: I heard you the first time, Boo. I told her I had a plane to catch.

BOO: Well, she still wants to talk.

JACK: I got an extra ticket, Mare.

BOO: Uncle, she's thinking about using her share of Babe's money to set up more halfway houses now. She wants you to get Tommy Hawk to lend them his name—

JACK: Oh, shit.

BOO: You're the real estate king.

JACK: Tommy Hawk Houses! I'll be back. Think about it, Mare. *(he exits)*

BOO: You wouldn't be serious about my uncle?

MARY: Hello, Miss Fisher. I'm Mary—

BOO: I know who you are.

(A heartbeat)

BOO: It's business first with him?

MARY: Look, it's probably nothing, okay? I don't know how it happened.

BOO: Why do you hang around here?

MARY: I just wanted to do a story about—

BOO: The Babe, the Babe. You people scare the vultures.

MARY: I only want to know the truth, okay?

BOO: Did you help my Ma with the kerosene?

MARY: It wasn't like that. It wasn't my fault.

BOO: "I don't know how it happened." Who the hell are you? What's in this for you? Why is it any of your business? You're a danger to ordinary people.

MARY: Look, people need to know.

BOO: People need to feel superior. 'Oh, we're getting somewhere now.' They're so fucking glad she's dead. Babe didn't belong in their story anyhow.

MARY: That's not it at all.

BOO: You or somebody else right now is writing it all up, explaining it all away. Then they'll just forget about her. And the whole muddle-headed Toward Utopia thing. She was all that was holding those jerks together.

MARY: Look, I'm sorry you feel that way but—

(The dreamy heartbeat starts)

BOO: Come on out of here. I got something to tell you.

(All the lights except the path pulse down with the heartbeats. BOO *leads* MARY *a little distance down the path)*

MARY: You're hurting me.

BOO: You don't know hurt. That's your problem. You don't know the half of it. A profound and paralyzing ignorance, okay?

MARY: It's not funny.

BOO: Funny? Of course it's funny. And you can't understand the half of it. Here's a joke. Who knows the most about Babe? Did you see that dame in black? Of course you did.

MARY: Who is she?

BOO: I thought you were the reporter? *(waving the piece of paper)* But you're clueless.

MARY: Give me that.

BOO: A boarding pass.

MARY: For a Miss—

BOO: Mary Oh.

MARY: What kind of joke is this?

BOO: Who, you'll notice, flew here from Hawaii.

MARY: I don't understand.

BOO: The story's just waiting for you, okay?

MARY: Tommy Hawk lives in Hawaii!

BOO: Wait. There's a quicker way to paradise.

MARY: You're ripping my coat.

BOO: You know what the Babe told me? This is even funnier.

MARY: Why should I listen to anything you say?

BOO: No reason. No reason at all.

MARY: Then thank you for your help. Jack! *(she exits along the path)*

BOO: This was just before she took off to go live with Jack and Tommy. For the Little People program? We was all sad and glad about it. Kids grow up and disappoint us. I mean that's what Ma told me. But Babe, she amazed us.

(The path begins to pulse with the heartbeats)

BOO
as BABE: Auntie, remember when I was little? When we first come to live with Granma out here in the bush? Remember how I got so lonesome out here at first with nobody to play with? I was a sulk that first winter, wasn't I? A genuine sulk. Well,,, Auntie, I used to all the time go walking in the bush. Even at night. Ya, even though you warned me about bears and skunks and stuff. I thought you was fooling. You was always teasing me, Auntie.

(Snow begins a gentle fall and the path fades)

BOO
as BABE: And then Auntie, remember how I got better? Can you guess why? That night I got lost. You guys gone to the village Christmas shopping. So, I was out walking, thinking about stuff Uncle Curly said about spirit and animal teachers, and thinking about how silly that stuff was, how can an animal teach, it can't even talk. And then I noticed it was bright, Auntie, like the moon and then some. But then I remembered it was cloudy, there wasn't no moon at all that night, and I turned around, Auntie, and there was a UFO there, ya, a UFO just floating there above me and the bare trees like a big balloon of light. And it was so pretty, Auntie, so full of bright turning rings and stuff—it looked like one of them things you use to measure where stars are?—I wasn't afraid when it come down around me like snow.

(The Milky Way fades in)

BOO
as BABE: And I saw there was this bear there, Auntie. Ya, a bear at the controls! And you're always giving me bear hugs, right? Well,,, Auntie, I heard that bear laugh! And the next thing I know we was rising up, and flying over the village, and then up through the clouds and, Auntie, we got almost to the moon afore we turned around and started heading back. And do you know how far that is? You look back here at a round blue ball and it's the earth and—

you don't know how much it looks like home. That's where it comes from, Auntie, that's where all this comes from. That's where I got my song. That's why I'm going to go there again someday, Auntie. Hey, that's what this is all for.

*(*BOO *catches some snowflakes in her open palm. Then the heartbeat stops and the Milky Way lights also go down)*

ACT TWO, SCENE TWO

(A heartbeat and a monitor comes on full of snow. A second heartbeat and the night city comes up to reveal TOMMY *Hawk playing to a camera in the shadows. His live image is on the monitor)*

TOMMY: The birth of this beautiful little baby girl child, it was fabulous, it was amazing, it was a very, very special event.

(A heartbeat and the night city and TOMMY *disappear and the image on the monitor flips into snow. Then one last beat and airplane interior night lights come up on* JACK, *sleeping, and* MARY, *seated next to him, fiddling with the buttons on the monitor)*

MARY: Oh, I can't hear a thing. Hello? Hello?

(A telecommunication format with identification logo and codes and an image of postcard stills of Honolulu comes up on the monitor accompanied by Hawaiian tourist music. A spot comes up to illuminate MARY *for the camera and the music softens)*

SYSTEM: *(over)* This is your automated Tele Presence system for the central Pacific. You have connected with the state of Hawaii. Aloha. A detailed weather forecast for tourist zones including Waikiki can be obtained by pushing one now. Arrival times for all scheduled airlines can be accessed by pushing two now. Reservations for all island and inter-island tours can be obtained by pushing three now. Information regarding visas for visits to the Homelands on the island of Hawaii can be obtained by pushing four now.

(MARY *pushes four)*

SYSTEM: *(over)* This is information for the Big Island. Please enter the name of the person or company you wish to visit. Please use a phonetic spelling for the names of Hawaiian nationals. For individuals, please enter the last or surname first, the first or personal name last. For companies, please enter the complete name—

(MARY *begins typing)*

SYSTEM: *(over)* Tee. Oh. Em. Em. Why. Space. Aitch. Ay. Double you. Kay. You wish to visit Tommy Hawk.

(A heartbeat)

SYSTEM: *(over)* Tommy Hawk Incorporated is a guest company of the Pele Homelands on the Big Island. One moment, please.

(The music comes up for a moment, then cuts out)

SYSTEM: *(over)* This call is being charged to the account of the *V. D. Oh Show*. Your name is Mary Oh. You are calling on Mister Jack Buck's special access code. Your call is being transferred now.

(A switch to the sound of surf and a real time view out a window of Hilo where it's sunrise)

(A heartbeat)

OPERATOR: *(over)* Hello from Hilo. Good grief, it's aloha in the morning. You coming to see the new eruption?

MARY: I'm calling for Tommy Hawk.

OPERATOR: *(over)* Oh, ha? Hey, it's early here. Coffee's not ready.

MARY: It's sort of an emergency.

OPERATOR: *(over)* Isn't the Hawk man away? He be sorry he missed the new lava flow. Excuse us. Something sad in Canada, did I hear?

MARY: The Crazy Horse. Babe Fisher was an old friend of his.

(A heartbeat)

OPERATOR: *(over)* Oh, ha! That poor kid. Well, somebody's always at the hole. Just a mo'. Here you go.

(The image on the monitor cuts a cartoon version of a tipi with a silly, hyped-up electronic tomtom riff, an excerpt from an old cheaply made opening for a kid's television show. The cartoon image dissolves into a full close-up of the BEAVER *puppet)*

BEAVER: Hello, little people!

MARY: Hello, I'm—

BEAVER: How are you today? How, how, how! I'm the Eager Beaver. I'm here to help you.

MARY: I'm calling for Tommy Hawk?

BEAVER: Can you say Eager Beaver? I'm from Canada. Can you say Canada?

MARY: Look, is Mister Hawk there?

BEAVER: My friends just call me Eager. Can you say Eager? Call me Eager and I'll take a message.

MARY: An answering program!

BEAVER: I'm not an answering program!

MARY: Mister Hawk, I know you were at Martha Fisher's funeral.

BEAVER: I am a real beaver!

MARY: Mister Hawk, I figured it out.

BEAVER: Call me Eager and I'll take a message.

MARY: I know you have a story for me.

(A heartbeat)

BEAVER: I am a real beaver!

MARY: Operator? Operator, hello.

(From the monitor comes the loud sound of a moose call, then the gallop of hooves. The noise rouses JACK*)*

MARY: Stewardess? I can't disconnect this stupid thing.

(In the image on the monitor one of the antlers of the Chocolate MOOSE *puppet comes into the background behind the* BEAVER*)*

MOOSE: *C'est qui?*

JACK: What the fuck—?

BEAVER: One of the little people.

MOOSE: *Merveillieux!*

(The camera pulls back to a two-shot of the puppets)

MARY: I'm trying to get an appointment.

MOOSE: *Bon* jo*ur, mes petits!* How, how how!

MARY: Mister Hawk, are you there?

*(*MOOSE *nods yes and* BEAVER *shakes his head no)*

JACK: It's better with him to just show up.

*(*MOOSE *and* BEAVER *look at each other)*

MARY: Look you—

(MOOSE *shakes her head no and* BEAVER *nods yes)*

JACK: He's a bit—creative, you know.

MARY: When is he expected?

BEAVER: It's all up in the air.

MOOSE: *En volant?*

BEAVER: We don't call him the Hawk for nothing!

JACK: The little faggot's liable to hide or run away.

MARY: I want to make an appointment to talk to Tommy Hawk.

JACK: He never asked me about no moose.

MARY: It's about Babe Fisher.

(The dreamy heartbeat begins)

BEAVER: You said the magic word!

MOOSE: The Babe!

(The image on the monitor dissolves to another camera that reveals TOMMY *Hawk standing beside the puppet platform, now in a complete Indian clown costume, including a cartoon-size corncob)*

TOMMY: How!

MARY: Mister Hawk, I want to talk to you—

TOMMY: *(tomahawking the camera with his corn cob)* How!

JACK: Save your breath. It's still part of the answering program.

TOMMY: *(to the camera)* Hello, little people, hello.

JACK: Look. The i.d. number.

TOMMY: This here's your Uncle Tommy. So, how are you today? How, how...

JACK: Fucking thing was recorded last week.

TOMMY: Hey, I'm here to tell a story, one I never told you before. One you all really want to know. That's why you called, why and how how how...

JACK: Turn it off.

TOMMY: Hey, it all starts out not even twenty-five years ago. Ya, not even a quarter century has come and gone since—

BEAVER: Shouldn't that be 'Many, many moons ago'?

MARY: I know it's about her.

TOMMY: *(to* BEAVER*)* No. Not this story. Understand?

JACK: He's fucked up the make up!

TOMMY: *(to the camera)* Not even a full quarter of this great twenty-first century has gone past now since the night, so dark and blizzardy, a good but poor woman brought a brand-new life into this cold old world. That spanking fresh life was a little baby girl child, little people. A little baby girl child.

(The airplane interior fades and is replaced by the path, JACK *and* MARY *lost in the shadows)*

TOMMY: And to that good but poor woman, that babe in her embracing arms had all the magical charms of the best of all possible Christmas presents.

BEAVER: Is this the event in the far north trapline tent?

MOOSE: *Ces contes Autochtone sont toutes les même.*

TOMMY: Now this gorgeous little baby girl child came into a mess of a world, a world where people were always asking each other: What the heck sort of world is this any way to bring a poor little innocent child into? To bring a poor little innocent child up in? What the hell sort of place of a planet is this, where all there are are all these liars and stealers everywhere you look, where there ain't no kind of kindness nowhere?

BEAVER: Some say people have always asked these questions.

MOOSE: *On a dit c'était toujours comme ça.*

BEAVER: Some people have no sense of occasion.

TOMMY: *(to the puppets)* Cut the crap. *(to the camera)* The birth of this beautiful little baby girl child, it was fabulous, it was amazing, it was a very, very special event.

BEAVER: It's true. I was there.

MOOSE: *Moi aussi.*

BEAVER: Something in the air...

TOMMY: How special, how fabulous that birth was!

MOOSE: *Voilà une étoile!*

BEAVER: I thought it was the moon—

TOMMY: For that sweet as corn, innocent little baby doll of a girl child was Barbara 'Babe' Fisher, as all you little people know. And all you little people have heard the story told: how her dear auntie and her wise granny found the babe and her good mother as they wandered lost in that cold and wild place, how they took them home, little people, took them home to a snug as a rug log house on the New Nations Reserve, how she grew up there through the years, beside that grand river, in the fabulously gorgeous light of sunshine and butterflies and the love of those three fine women, more beautiful and sweet each and every day.

MOOSE: *Comme le maïs*, yes?

(The path fades and the night city comes up)

TOMMY: Ya, little people, ya. Like the corn and the beans and the squash, just like them.

BEAVER: How, how, how!

TOMMY: Well, I tell you now, little ones, that I was there then, I was there, on the New Nations, ya, working, ya, working in their brand new television station, in their spanking new public relations. Ya, your Uncle Tommy was there. It was way before I had wings. And I tell you now I saw her then and there and I thought, ya. But what did I think? When her uncle—no, her momma first brought her to me, ya, I was honoured and I figured, ya, she would be the first and the best of the Little People.

BEAVER: Uncle, the story.

TOMMY: I thought that. I did, kids. And I tell you, kids, she inspired me. Watching her grow—what are the words?—'tall and sweet as the corn, and as full of power.' One of her songs? Ya. What else do you want me to say, little people? You know she used to bring me coffee when we worked. At the music.

Little people, we learned to dance and sing and to listen. Oh, yes. Her granny. How now...? How, how, how many generations? Care for them. That's what we got to do. That's our job now. Nurture and spare no expense. All them dollars and no sense! Ha ha! How how how I loved my very own little baby doll girl.

MOOSE: Uncle?

(The night city fades and the Milky Way comes up)

TOMMY: What you want? The princess should have an Indian name! Shirley Temple Red? Whatever that means. Princess, I guess—Oh, little people, Babe, she—How, how, how? I knew the Crazy Horse was bad. Medicine, crystal gazers. Pee aitch dee. Piled higher and deeper, Curly said. Her momma so proud. What momma? How did this—Later. Later, she said to me.

BEAVER: Tommy? Tom, you all—? How can we use this? It's sort of all over the place.

TOMMY: They want to know.

BEAVER: But it isn't Uncle Tommy Hawk. It's going to need a lot of editing. The language—

TOMMY: This is what they get.

BEAVER: How can we use this?

TOMMY: What do I pay you for?

BEAVER: It's not very funny.

(The dreamy heartbeat stops)

TOMMY: *(tomahawking the camera with his corncob)* How! How! How!

(The screen image cuts to Hilo again. Then the Tele Presence logo flashes on screen and the voice of the SYSTEM *comes on)*

SYSTEM: *(over)* Thank you, Mary Oh, for using Tele Presence. A charge of nine zero six zero dollars and zero five cents—

JACK: What a piece of crap.

SYSTEM: *(over)* —has been debited from your expense account with the *V. D. Oh Show*. This includes a charge of one zero zero six dollars and five five cents tax.

JACK: He's just slit his own throat.

SYSTEM: *(over)* Have a good day, wherever you may be.

*(*JACK *turns the monitor off. A heartbeat and the Milky Way flares and goes to blackout)*

ACT TWO, SCENE THREE

(The dreamy heartbeats with the petroglyphs pulsing in and out. RICKY, *a shadow in the shadows, on the second beat, turns a flashlight on, uses it as a blinding search light)*

RICKY: No wonder she became a star! No wonder she stole our hearts. No wonder she disappeared!

(The flashlight and petroglyphs go out and the heartbeats stop as the monitor blares on: Fred FACE *is reporting. The monitor shows the clip of the haloed, spinning shuttle)*

FACE: —confirmed that yesterday morning's mission of mercy to the Crazy Horse has also not met with success.

*(*TOMMY, *half lit by the monitor's glow, is spinning himself around and around. Parts of his clown costume—his corncob, his nose, a glove, a shoe—keep flying off. The monitor shows a panel worried scientists talking to reporters)*

FACE: Scientific delegates to the United Nations have expressed increasing concern because the intense magnetic field that has developed around the Crazy Horse has begun to distort the orbits of nearby satellites, including two in geosynchronous orbits.

(The monitor shows a computer simulation of satellites drifting out of their places in the world's communications network and that network breaking down while the satellites begin to orbit the shuttle)

FACE: Unless the situation can be soon rectified, delegates warn that disruptions in the World Com-Net could rival those of major sunspot activity in the last decade.

(The monitor shows images of mobs rioting and looting, the U.N. building in the background)

FACE: It raises questions about the possible threat to the world's peace and economy from areas left outside communication control. The ambassador of the United States has assured the assembly that no new disturbances are expected in Manhattan.

(The monitor shows a computer simulation of the shuttle nearly hitting the partially constructed rings of the Moon Two)

FACE: No one at the launch facility has been available to comment on questions about the Crazy Horse's proximity to the shell of the Moon Two space station and scientists are refusing to speculate about what action will be taken to solve this problem.

(The monitor shows a simulation of a missile hitting the shuttle and blowing it apart in a spray of debris)

*(*TOMMY*'s security system flashes warning lights and then cuts onto the monitor with the silly, hyped-up electronic tomtom riff from the television introduction and a close-up image of* MARY *and* JACK *in bright tropical exterior light.* TOMMY *collapses out of his spin to the ground. He is naked except for the clown white he now wipes from his face)*

MARY: What is this place?

JACK: The little bugger's hideout.

MARY: But what is it?

JACK: Lava flow tube. Volcano blew this way about twenty years ago.

MARY: Lava? But it's big enough to fit the shuttle in.

JACK: The clown's got a studio inside. And I was the fool who let him build it. *(to the camera)* Tommy, you shit, I know you're there.

*(*TOMMY *pushes his costume down a hole in the rock floor)*

MARY: But we're so close to the volcano.

(The hole burps flame)

JACK: *(pushes the door button and the tomtom riff plays again)* The flow's miles from here now.

*(*TOMMY *starts putting street clothes on)*

MARY: Are you sure? I smell sulphur.

JACK: Vog. Volcanic fog. The whole island reeks. What a hole.

MARY: Why doesn't he answer?

(JACK *presses the button again and the again the riff plays)*

JACK: Shit, I hate that tune.

MARY: Could he be asleep?

JACK: Or out watching the goddess Pele creating the world. He just loves the fucking volcano.

MARY: What if he's hurt?

JACK: *(he pushes the door button again)* What a good idea.

(TOMMY *turns the sound of the tomtom off in mid riff. He finishes dressing by putting on a coonskin hat and suddenly he is* RICKY *Raccoon again)*

JACK: I'm sure there was an escape route on the blue-prints.

MARY: I saw a path back there.

JACK: Wait here in case he pops up.

MARY: Okay.

JACK: I'll break in the back way.

(JACK *walks out of the image and* MARY *waves goodbye. After a moment she presses the door button again and* RICKY *presses a button to answer)*

RICKY: Hi ho, how are you? You heard the latest? Tommy Hawk is dead. Ya. Isn't that sad? Ain't that just too fucking bad? Ha! Long live me! Tommy Hawk is dead. Long live Ricky!—

MARY: Hello? Hello, Mister Hawk?

RICKY: —Tommy Hawk is dead and it's too fucking bad. Ain't that sad? Long live me! Tommy—

MARY: Jack? He's here. Jack!

RICKY: —Hawk is dead and it's too fucking bad. Long live Ricky! *(he presses another button)*

(The dreamy heartbeat starts as all the lights go out and RICKY *disappears and the image of* MARY *warps and she drops out of it as if into a trap door. The monitor flips to images from* MARY*'s virtuo show with her dancing and suddenly a second* MARY *falls by the dancing* MARY. JACK *enters)*

JACK: Tommy? Tommy, where the fuck are you? I know you're here, you little shit. Come out, come out. You little faggot.

(The monitor starts to flip through images from earlier in the play—including the petroglyphs, the ghost face JACK *saw in the shuttle window, the night city, the Milky Way, some shuttle flight and disaster images and animation—and* MARY *falls through each one)*

JACK: You can't fuck around with my programming. Tommy Hawk was my concept! *(noticing the images*

of MARY *on the monitor)* Mary? What the hell—? Hawk? Hawk? Where the fuck are—

(The monitor image cuts to an extreme close-up of RICKY *and* JACK *stumbles back from it and falls down the hole in the rock. The hole belches flame and then a spot comes up on* MARY *lost in front of the monitor)*

MARY: What's going on?

RICKY: What's going on on on on!

MARY: Who are you?

RICKY: Who are you you you you!

MARY: What do you want?

RICKY: What do you want want want want!

MARY: Stop it!

(All lights go out as the image warps and RICKY *drops out of it as if into a trap door. The monitor starts to replay the images of* MARY *dancing, the petroglyphs, the shuttle ghost face, the night city, the Milky Way et cetera as a loop in the background while* MARY *in extreme close-up finds herself trapped in the monitor and pushes at the screen as a spot glares up on* RICKY *standing facing the monitor)*

MARY: What's going on?

RICKY: Who! What! When! Where! Why! *(he mimics* MARY*'s dancing image)*

MARY: What do you want? Who are you?

RICKY: Who! What! When! Where! Why! *(he starts spinning himself around and around)* Who! What! When! Where! Why!

MARY: Listen to me! What do you want? What do you want?

RICKY: Who! What! When! Where! Why! Who what when where why! *(his spinning accelerates)* How how how how!

MARY: Stop it!

RICKY: How how how how! How how how how! How how how how!

MARY: Stop it! Stop it! Stop it!

(All lights out as MARY *drops out of the monitor and* RICKY *falls out of his spin. The heartbeat stops. The monitor fills with the night city. A moon light comes up slowly on* RICKY*)*

RICKY: No news, that's good news, right? Right? I keep my mouth shut and you can't get a hold on me. You don't know what to think, what to feel. You can't get me. That's what you want to do, that's what you're here for. You want to know how he feels. How how how the famous Indian host of the long-running Tommy Hawk and the Little Fuckers feels now now now that the little people are dead. Tommy's oh so delicious, you want to eat

him up, just like you did with them little folks. But it's too late for that, cuz he was one of them little buggers too, ya, Tommy Hawk, he's gone like a fart, gone west, passed over, up in smoke. And there's nobody in here but us Raccoons. And you don't want to know how how how we feel now, do you? You don't want to know what we think, do you? We aren't Indian enough, are we? Or are we like too Indian for you to chew? Are you hungry enough now finally to eat anything? Are you? Are you? Well, chew on this. Sorry if it's kind of wooden. It's not news but it's good. The Raccoon was alone in the city. Don't know why. Let's say he thought the lights was pretty. Let's say his momma got run over by some drunk. Let's say his brother with the bright dark eyes one day did a dance at the end of a rope. Was it an Indian dance? A fairy dance? Something like that. Ya, the Raccoon was alone and hungry, he would have got stoned if he'd had the money. He would maybe even have tried the dance himself if he'd had the guts. Fairies can't grant themselves wishes, eh? Hey, let's come right out and say the Raccoon then wanted to be dead. But then this Indian girl, this Indian girl with bright dark eyes, said, Hey, little brother, have you seen my sister? And he thought he had.

(The night city image on the monitor cross-fades to the petroglyphs)

RICKY: What do you think about babies with bright dark eyes? Are you in favour of them? I am. I'd do anything to look after them. You can't let the cannibals get at them. Hey, that's what it's like in the big

town. You got to look after your own. Hey, I'd even become an Uncle Tomahawk. Would you like a cigar?

(The monitor cuts to a silent image of Fred FACE *reporting and then to another of a missile being launched)*

RICKY: It's so nice to have a niece around the house. Let's say the Raccoon took the baby in. It was a hole under an old theatre where the fairies boogied in their rings. Where the fairies went to get bombed. And those who knew the Babe was down there were called Darling, Dear, Bitch and Mary, fairy godmothers all.

(The monitor shows a silent image of a distant, star bright missile hitting the shuttle and blowing it apart in a flare of light)

RICKY: And they all conspired to take care of her and give her presents and blessings. And you know she slept in a trunk full of boas and bearskin—bare skin?—for years. No wonder she became a star! No wonder she stole our hearts. No wonder she disappeared!

(The monitor image whites out and then MARY*'s face appears in an extreme close-up, pressed against the glass, but then quickly the monitor sparks and goes dead as the spot on* RICKY *goes out. The petroglyphs flare and then fade to black)*

ACT TWO, SCENE FOUR

(The dreamy heartbeat in darkness for four beats, then the night city pulses in and a spot comes up on the large piece of metallic debris from the Crazy Horse, now mounted on a stone pedestal as a monument. The heartbeat stops and then the sounds of distant surf and insects fade in. Then the monitor blares on with the extreme close-up of MARY*'s face pressed against the glass and then cuts to clips of* MARY *dancing on her virtuo show as Fred* FACE *reporting blares on)*

FACE: —the centre of a complex controversy. It is Miss Oh who, of course, has become the primary suspect in the still unexplained disappearances six months ago—

(The monitor shows footage of JACK *and* TOMMY *on the set of The Little People show, celebrating their tenth anniversary)*

FACE: —of Big Buck Virtuo-Show Productions owner and president Jack Buck and of the popular host of children's television, Thomas Hawk. Harry Smith, Los Angeles Chief of Police, recently had this to say:

(The image on the monitor cuts to the CHIEF *looking concerned and uncomfortable)*

CHIEF: We don't want to make this into like more than it is but sure, Mister Buck was a pretty important guy around here. Ya, like my task force already has looked into, like, the woman's background. Hey, I mean she was there when the Crazy Horse blew and when, like, Missus Fisher burned. I don't like to sound superstitious or that but it's like we could have ourselves a regular Typhoon Mary here.

(The image on the monitor cuts back to Fred FACE*)*

FACE: Chief Smith stated that it is a video-recorded fact that Mary Oh was last seen in the company of Mister Buck and that the pair were en route to Hawaii and intended to visit Mister Hawk.

(The image on the monitor cuts back to the CHIEF*)*

CHIEF: I am told this is, like, a classic pattern. Like, someone who lives vicariously, like, off the famous. Past individuals has proved dangerous. Ya, we are attempting to answer those questions. Is she a stalker! Like, that sure is one of those questions. No, the producers of the *V. D. Oh Show* deny that she ever had any like real connections to—

(The image on the monitor cuts back to Fred FACE*)*

FACE: And this has just come in. Mary Oh has been located. She is on the New Nations Reserve. She has been given sanctuary in the the Fisher Community Entertainment Centre. It is Barbara Fisher Buck, secretary for the Council of the New Nations, who is speaking for them today:

(The monitor shows BARBARA *in close-up from the news conference. Dusk colours come up on* LARRY *and* CLARISSE *near the monument, waiting to be shot by cameraman* NICKY *who watches the monitor)*

BARBARA: Yes, our medicine women confirmed it. In her second trimester. The morning sickness? Over weeks ago—and now she's got this glow. Yes, that right, Mary's carrying Jack's child. We're all so excited about it. Well, of course I mean Jack Buck. You haven't been paying attention, have you? Excuse me? Yes, we know that you guys think that, but we don't see that she had anything to do with it. And besides, we can't just go turning the mothers of our babies over to foreigners. Enough's enough. Our chief tells me we don't even have a treaty with you guys anymore. So, stuff like—what do you call it, extradition?—that's not going to happen. That's right. See what paying attention can do? And besides, it wouldn't be good for the baby if Mary had to go to jail right now.

(The monitor image cuts back to the FACE. NICKY *does a countdown as his spotlight comes up)*

FACE: And now we take you to the recently unveiled monument to the memory of the crew of the shuttle Crazy Horse in the Merritt Island International Wildlife Sanctuary for an interview about a related story.

*(*NICKY *signals to* LARRY *as the monitor cuts to a two-shot of* LARRY *and* CLARISSE*)*

LARRY: Hello, Fred. I'm here with Clarisse Chrisjohn, a friend of Babe Fisher's family.

CLARISSE: I like the suit, Larry.

LARRY: Mizz Chrisjohn, we don't have a lot of time.

CLARISSE: Folks, I'm here at the memorial to the crew of the Crazy Horse—

*(*LARRY *steps out of the shot.* NICKY *moves* CLARISSE *into close-up)*

CLARISSE: —to honour the memory of Special Flight Officer Barbara the Babe. So, today we're establishing The Babe Fisher Foundation. 'We' means her relations, friends, the Toward Utopia Party and the governments of eighteen Native nations of the New World. And we're negotiating with a bunch of other Native nations worldwide so as to make the Babe foundation part of their national programs too. And we're even answering inquiries from the Princi-pality of Monaco, believe it or not.

LARRY: So far, so good.

CLARISSE: —It is the Babe Foundation's mandate to encourage governments and societies worldwide to re-establish an extended structure for the family in order to insure the welfare of our children and the planet. Our children are not for sale.

(The SISTER *enters)*

CLARISSE: —Indigenous governments like the Maori of New Zealand and the Hopi of North America have offered to help us find our balance. The Foundation wishes to resist the commodification of human—who wrote this crap?

LARRY: Hurry up!

CLARISSE: The Foundation today will prove its commitment to this effort by opening so-called half-way houses in twenty five cities in the Americas alone but its efforts will not be half-way. The Foundation's immediately instituting legal proceedings to adopt street youth into the participating families, clans and Nations.

SISTER: Excuse me.

LARRY: Lady, we're live!

SISTER: Okay, okay.

CLARISSE: —The Foundation believes that we are all Indians.

(The monitor cuts back to Fred FACE*)*

LARRY: Or we were.

CLARISSE: —Welcome to the tribe...

LARRY: *(to* CLARISSE*)* They cut you off.

FACE: Thank you, Larry, for that most interesting report.

CLARISSE: *(to* FACE*)* Fuck you.

LARRY: We're dead now.

CLARISSE: Sorry, Sister.

LARRY: My pink slip's in the mail.

SISTER: Like you need another one.

FACE: And finally, on a most exciting note, it is now confirmed that the orbit of the space station has been stabilized.

SISTER: I could have told you that would happen.

CLARISSE: Just what do you think you're doing here?

(On the screen, a view from space appears: distantly, indistinctly, the rise around the limb of the Earth of the space station, the Moon Two. NICKY *begins packing his equipment)*

LARRY: Who is this?

FACE: Last week's top secret shuttle mission to the Moon Two was completed without any problems according to a spokesperson for the Kennedy Space Centre—

CLARISSE: The ever-popular— *(removing the Sister's wimple)*

LARRY: Mary!

FACE: —The four-day shuttle mission also retrieved, repaired and replaced into their proper orbits the last pair of satellites which are part of the Com-Net.

(The monitor shows Fred FACE *reporting)*

SISTER: *(putting the wimple back on)* Don't let on.

FACE: It is the professional ease with which today's fuelling and firing have been accomplished that will revitalize the failing spirit of the space program.

*(*NICKY *pulls a plug and the monitor goes dark)*

LARRY: Mo? Oh, they got security all over the place.

*(*NICKY *exits with some equipment)*

SISTER: I wanted to see the monument, okay?

CLARISSE: The Council stuck its neck out for you, young lady.

SISTER: I wanted to hear you make the announcement too. Curly let me hide in the back and I'm just so sleepy these days.

CLARISSE: He's got no say! I'm in charge of your security. Come on. We can't have them get you now. *(she exits)*

LARRY: They really are watching us. Jack was a big deal.

SISTER: So, I'll go right home now.

LARRY: They have to find out what the story is or fry someone trying.

SISTER: I'm here now, Larry.

LARRY: So, what do you think, little missus? Clarisse calls it the wreck of hope. Four months of meetings, two million bucks and it's still a pile of junk.

*(*NICKY *enters and signals for the* SISTER *to come and then exits)*

LARRY: You better go.

SISTER: I was one of the Little People once.

(A heartbeat)

SISTER: We were friends.

LARRY: Mo, you never met her. She was better guarded than the queen.

SISTER: Well, I think I know what that's like.

LARRY: Mo, Jack was a big deal and now so are you. Hey, who else has the luck to be knocked up with, not by, a billionaire?

SISTER: It's not funny. Well, maybe a little.

LARRY: You better go.

SISTER: Okay. Visit me?

(NICKY *enters, signals and finishes packing his equipment)*

LARRY: Would I ignore my baby sister? Hey, we got that virtuo play to finish.

SISTER: Talk about a long-lasting relationship.

LARRY: There's a longer one on your horizon. Come on. *(to NICKY)* I'll see you later. I'm going to ride them to the airport.

(NICKY *nods assent.* LARRY *and the* SISTER *exit.* NICKY *checks to see that he is alone, then digs a raccoon cap out of his case and, putting it on, becomes* RICKY *again. The dreamy heartbeat begins distantly.* RICKY *wanders over to the Crazy Horse monument and starts to walk around it.* BOO *steps out from behind it)*

BOO: Hello, little brother.

RICKY: Shit, Boo, you freaked me. What you doing here?

BOO: Thought I'd take a look myself. It ain't exactly Mount Rushmore.

RICKY: You look good.

BOO: I'm alive.

RICKY: Ya. Did you see that Moon Two thing?

BOO: Ya. It looks just like—

RICKY: That toy the fairy godmothers hung up on the Babe's cradleboard!

BOO: She ever tell you her UFO story?

RICKY: Ya. One weird kid. Do all parents have these problems?

BOO: I been thinking about what Uncle Jack and Aunt Babsy would have made of her.

RICKY: Miss Indian North America, probably.

BOO: But wasn't this nuts? She could have had a regular life.

RICKY: Her? Little Babe Fisher? Hey, I bet she's got one now. Ya, she's alive and laughing in New Zealand. The UFO story's true, that's how it happened. Her alien bear hugged her out in time.

BOO: Ya. And we all got this whole ugly mess together as a plot so she could get out of having another dinner with the Prime Minister.

RICKY: Life can be rough that way. Ya, it sounds like her.

BOO: Hey, look.

(A yellow butterfly is shifting on top of the monument)

(The dreamy heartbeating drum grows closer and the butterfly takes flight and wanders along where the path appears)

(The butterfly disappears into a shadow as the other pulsing places, the projected petroglyphs and city and Milky Way, also return, in their cycling, and

the space station, Moon Two, rises above a clearing bank of clouds. It's moon bright and large, a spectacle of rings and squares, spheres and cubes—a gigantic high technology astrolabe, a turning tesseract, a future spirit catcher)

(And along comes BABE *again, dawdling as always, trailing her red balloon. And as before,* CLARISSE *and* JACK, *and then* BARBARA *and* MARY, *and then* BOO *and* RICKY, *appear facing* BABE. *And again she dances a few steps. But now when she loses her hold on the balloon and the drum hesitates, the other characters turn and talk to each other)*

CLARISSE: Like it looked alive and I remember I wondered if it was like holding its breath or maybe was just moving slow so I couldn't tell for sure in them shadows.

JACK: But shit, then the Babe's face was there at the window—

BARBARA: She told me that little man lived there?

JACK: —and all them guys gone.

MARY: I was there.

BOO: We was all sad and glad about it.

CLARISSE: Like them cracks was opening up like mouths.

RICKY: No wonder she became a star!

CLARISSE: Like the mouth of that baby.

JACK: And then it was the sun at that window.

BARBARA: She said he was hiding there in the grove.

MARY: I was at the Space Centre, you know, when it happened.

BOO: Kids grow up and usually they disappoint us.

BARBARA: You know something?

RICKY: No wonder she stole our hearts.

BOO: But Babe, she amazed us.

MARY: I never got to meet her. I wanted to.

RICKY: No wonder she disappeared!

BARBARA: I believed her. I believed her.

(And all the lights but the path fade down as they talk)

(And the balloon lifts away and BABE*'s eyes follow it with longing. Then the drum somewhere ahead begins to play again and* BABE *hears it and begins to dance wholeheartedly along the fading path)*

(And the progress toward the sky of the balloon stops, fades to the stars. And then there's a last glimpse of the city lights, of the Milky Way, of the path and then of the petroglyphs, those images of men, women, boats, bears, turtles, Nanabush. And then in the darkness, the heartbeating drum stops)

END OF THE PLAY

Kyotopolis was produced by the Graduate Centre for the Study of Drama of the University of Toronto, directed by Colin Taylor, 17-28 March 1993.

The author thanks the Canada Council, the Graduate Drama Centre and the Art Studio of the Banff Centre for the Arts for their support during the development of this play. He is especially grateful to Colin Taylor for his continuing passion for the "rich and strange."

This book is entirely printed on FSC certified paper.